COUNSELING OLDER PERSONS

COUNSELING
OLDER PERSONS

An Annotated Bibliography

Compiled by
**Valerie L. Schwiebert
and Jane E. Myers**

Bibliographies and Indexes in Gerontology, Number 26
Erdman B. Palmore, Series Adviser

GREENWOOD PRESS
Westport, Connecticut • London

Library of Congress Cataloging-in-Publication Data

Schwiebert, Valerie L.
    Counseling older persons : an annotated bibliography / compiled by
Valerie L. Schwiebert and Jane E. Myers.
       p.   cm.—(Bibliographies and indexes in gerontology, ISSN
0743–7560 ; no. 26)
    Includes indexes.
    ISBN 0–313–29277–9 (alk. paper)
    1. Aged—Services for—United States—Bibliography. 2. Aged—
Counseling of—United States—Bibliography. I. Myers, Jane E.
II. Title. III. Series.
Z7164.04S38 1995
016.3626'6'0973—dc20   94–44351

British Library Cataloguing in Publication Data is available.

Library of Congress Catalog Card Number: 94–44351
ISBN: 0–313–29277–9
ISSN: 0743–7560

First published in 1995

Greenwood Press, 88 Post Road West, Westport, CT 06881
An imprint of Greenwood Publishing Group, Inc.

Printed in the United States of America

The paper used in this book complies with the
Permanent Paper Standard issued by the National
Information Standards Organization (Z39.48–1984).

10 9 8 7 6 5 4 3 2 1

Contents

Series Foreword

The annotated bibliographies in this series provide answers to the fundamental question, "What is known?" Their purpose is simple, yet profound: to provide comprehensive reviews and references for the work done in various fields of gerontology. They are based on the fact that it is no longer possible for anyone to comprehend the vast body of research and writing in even one sub-specialty without years of work.

This fact has become true only in recent years. When I was an undergraduate (Class of '52) I think no one at Duke had even heard of gerontology. Almost no one in the world was identified as a gerontologist. Now there are over 6,000 professional members of the Gerontological Society of America. When I was an undergraduate there were no courses in gerontology. Now there are thousands of courses offered by most major (and many minor) colleges and universities. When I was an undergraduate there was only one gerontological journal (the *Journal of Gerontology* begun in 1945). Now there are over forty professional journals and several dozen books in gerontology published each year.

The reasons for this dramatic growth are well known: the dramatic increase in numbers of aged, the shift from family to public responsibility for the security and care of the elderly, the recognition of aging as a "social problem", and the growth of science in general. It is less well known that this explosive growth in knowledge has developed the need for new solutions to the old problem of comprehending and "keeping up" with a field of knowledge. The old indexes and library card catalogues have become increasingly inadequate for the job. On-line computer indexes and abstracts are one solution but make no evaluative selections nor organize sources logically as is done here. These annotated bibliographies are also more widely available than on-line computer indexes.

These bibliographies will obviously be useful for students, teachers, and researchers who need to know what research has (or has not) been done in their field. This particular bibliography will also be useful to mental health workers and counselors. The annotations contain enough information so that the user usually does not have to search out the original articles.

In the past, the "review of literature" has often been haphazard and was rarely comprehensive, because of the large investment of time (and money) that would be required by a truly comprehensive review. Now, using these bibliographies, researchers and others concerned with this topic can be more confident that they are not duplicating past efforts and "reinventing the wheel". It may well become standard and expected practice for researchers to consult such bibliographies, even before they start their research.

The research relevant to counseling older persons has become a large and rapidly growing field, especially in the last few decades. This is attested to by the 481 references in this bibliography, and by the wide variety of disciplines represented here. Thus this volume will be useful to counselors, other professionals, and researchers in many different fields.

The authors have done an outstanding job of covering the recent literature and organizing it into easily accessible form. Not only are the entries organized into 9 chapters and numerous sub-sections, but there is a preface and comprehensive subject and author indexes.

Thus one can look for relevant material in this volume in several ways: (1) look up a given subject in the subject index; (2) look up a given author in the author index; or (3) turn to the chapter and subsection that covers the subject in which you are interested.

The authors are exceptionally well-qualified to produce this bibliography. Myers has long been a specialist in this area, has done significant research, and has published several articles on counseling. Schwiebert has also published in this area.

So it is with great pleasure that we add this bibliography to our series. We believe you will find this volume to be the most useful comprehensive, and easily accessible reference work in its field. I will appreciate any comments you care to send me.

Erdman B. Palmore
Center for the Study of Aging and Human Development
Box 3003, Duke University Medical Center
Durham, NC 27710

Preface

Demographic changes in the population over age 65 are having a profound impact on American society. At the turn of the century, 4.1% of the United States population was age 65 and over. By 1988, this number had grown to 12.4% of the total population (U.S. Administration on Aging, 1989). Population projections indicate this group will continue to grow to 21.8% of the total population by 2030 (U.S. Bureau of the Census, 1984). These changes do not solely reflect a growth in numbers in this segment of the population but a growth in proportion as well. In the last 20 years, the over 65 population increased by 24% compared to a 6% increase in those under age 65. Of the over age 65 group, those age 85 and older are now, and are expected to remain, the fastest growing age segment in the total population. Furthermore, the number of persons aged 85 or older has increased 23 times since 1900; the number of persons aged 75 to 84 has increased 12 times; and the number of persons aged 65 to 74 has increased 8 times. It is estimated that by the year 2010, there will be 6.8 million persons over age 85 or 2.4% of the total population (U.S. Administration on Aging, 1989).

The circumstances of later life create both challenges and opportunities for aging persons. Most cope successfully with the changes of aging, however, some older persons require assistance to cope and adapt successfully. As the older population grows, the sheer numbers of persons in need of mental health assistance may be expected to grow dramatically. As a result, mental health counselors in all settings may be called upon to serve older persons and their families in some capacity. Therefore, it is essential that all counselors be familiar with the needs of older persons and their families and counseling interventions which will be beneficial in helping to meet those needs (Myers, 1989a, 1989b, 1990).

Interest in older persons within the counseling profession has developed only within the past 15-20 years. As the lifespan has increased, counselors have moved from a primary focus on school populations to an equally strong emphasis on community-based programs addressing the mental health concerns of persons across the lifespan (Palmo, Weikel & Brooks, 1987). Counselors have begun to work with older persons, and the question has emerged of whether and how such work is different from counseling with any other population. Recently, Burns and Taube (1990) noted that the extent of mental health needs does not seem to change with age, while Knight (1989) determined that psychotherapy is as effective with older persons as with people of any age group. Thompson (1987) determined that age is not a factor in therapy outcome, hence older persons can benefit from counseling to the same extent as persons of younger ages.

Waters (1984) identified both similarities *and* differences in counseling with older and younger persons. Numerous authors have written concerning specialized techniques for use with older people (e.g., Brammer, 1985; Burnside, 1984), presumably based on different needs of this population. A major difference is the reluctance of older persons to seek counseling (Cohen, 1977; Gaitz, 1974). In addition, the reluctance of therapists to treat older people has been documented (Poggi & Berland, 1985). Kunkel and Williams (1991) identified an additional barrier to services as the lack of research-informed theoretical perspectives on how to provide mental health services most effectively to older people and how to encourage older people to use such services. As a group, older people are substantially underserved by mental health practitioners (Flemming, Rickards, Santos, & West, 1986; Roybal, 1988), in part because of negative attitudes (Piggrem & Schmidt, 1982) and in part due to lack of specialized training (Myers & Blake, 1986).

Specialized training opportunities in counseling services for older persons have increased substantially over the past 15 years (Myers, Loesch, & Sweeney, 1990). These include both pre- and in-service training programs. Preservice preparation has been affected by the development of standards for training in gerontological counseling. The Council for Accreditation of Counseling and Related Educational Programs (CACREP) approved accreditation standards for training programs in gerontological counseling in 1992 (CACREP, 1994). The National Board for Certified Counselors (NBCC) approved the National Certified Gerontological Counselor (NCGC) credential in 1991, a national board specialty certification for counselors who work with older people. Both the training standards and the certification were based on a nationally endorsed statement of competencies for training gerontological counselors (Myers & Sweeney, 1990). These competencies were used as the basis for identifying articles for inclusion in this annotated bibliography. In other words, we chose citations which can contribute to competency-based knowledge and skills in gerontological counseling.

The purpose of this annotated bibliography is to provide counselors and other mental health professionals with a compilation of state-of-the-art references in the area of counseling older persons. These citations are categorized into several sections for ease of reference including: normative experience of aging, older persons with impairments, needs and services for older persons, population and special situations, techniques for counseling older persons, ethics in gerontological counseling, practica and internships in gerontology, and pharmacology. In addition, to providing information related to each area, a brief survey of the number of citations in each area (or the lack thereof) will assist the reader in identifying areas which have received little research attention to date. Since aging is a universal condition, knowledge of the current state-of-the-art is essential for the development of policy, research, and action which will benefit all individuals.

REFERENCES

Brammer, L. (1985). Counseling and quality of life for older adults: Beating the odds. Educational Perspectives, 23, 3-16.

Burns, B.J. & Tube, C.A. (1990). Mental health services in general medical care and in nursing homes. In B.S. Fogel, A. Furino, & G. Gottlieb (Eds.), Protecting minds at risk. Washington, DC: American Psychiatric Association.

Burnside, I. (1984). Working with the elderly: Group processes and techniques. Monterey, CA: Wadsworth.

Cohen, G. (1977). Mental health services and the elderly: Needs and options. In S. Steury & M.L. Black (Eds.), Readings in psychotherapy with older people. Rockville, MD: National Institutes of Mental Health.

Council for Accreditation of Counseling and Related Educational Programs. (1994). Accreditation standards and procedures manual. Alexandria, VA: Author.

Flemming, A.S., Rickards, L.D., Santos, J.F., & West, P.R. (1986). Report of a survey of community mental health centers (Vol. 1). Washington, DC: White House Conference on Aging.

Gaitz, C. (1974). Barriers to the delivery of psychiatric services to the elderly. Gerontologist, 14, 210-214.

Knight, B.G. (1989). Outreach with the elderly: Community education, assessment, and therapy. New York: New York University Press.

Kunkel, M.A., & Williams, C. (1991). Age and expectations about counseling: Two methodological perspectives. Journal of Counseling and Development, 70, 314-320.

Myers, J.E. (1989a). Adult children, aging parents. Alexandria, VA: American Counseling Association.

Myers, J.E. (1989b). Infusing gerontological counseling into counselor preparation: Curriculum guide. Alexandria, VA: American Association for Counseling and Development.

Myers, J.E., & Blake, R. (1986). Employment of gerontological counseling graduates: A follow-up study. Personnel and Guidance Journal, 62(6), 333-335.

Myers, J.E., Loesch, T.J., & Sweeney, T.J. (1991). Trends in gerontological counselor preparation. Counselor Education and Supervision, 30(3), 194-204.

Myers, J.E., & Sweeney, T.J. (1990). Gerontological competencies for counselors and human development professionals. Alexandria, VA: American Association for Counseling and Development.

Palmo, A.J., Weikel, W.J., & Brooks, D.K. (Eds.). Foundations of mental health counseling. St. Louis: C.C. Thomas.

Piggrem, G.W., & Schmidt, L. (1982). Counseling the elderly. Counseling and Human Development, 14, 1-12.

Poggi, R.G., & Berland, D.I. (1985). The therapists' reactions to the elderly. The Gerontologist, 25(5), 508-513.

Roybal, E.R. (1988). Mental health and aging: The need for an expanded federal response. American Psychologist, 43, 189-194.

Thompson, L. (1987). Comparative effectiveness of psychotherapy for depressed elders. Journal of Consulting and Clinical Psychology, 55(3), 385-390.

United States Administration on Aging. (1989). A profile of older Americans. Washington, DC: Author.

United States Bureau of the Census. (1984). Current population reports (Series P-25, No. 952). Washington, DC: Author.

Waters, E. (1984). Building on what you know: Individual and group counseling for older people. The Counseling Psychologist, 12(2), 52-64.

Acknowledgments

The authors would like to acknowledge the assistance of Erdman B. Palmore, series editor, and Mildred Vasan, social and behavioral sciences editor at Greenwood Press for their support in the development of this bibliography.

We would also like to express our appreciation for the counsel and instruction provided by Deb Holderness, friend and colleague, in the computerization and preparation of this manuscript. Her advice and support were much appreciated.

Finally, we would like to thank our graduate assistants, Theresa Flight and Laura Klutz-Wachsmuth for their assistance in the development of the library computer searches and organization of the resulting abstracts.

1

Normative Experience of Aging

1   **Brown, M.T. (1989). A cross-sectional analysis of self-disclosure patterns. <u>Journal of Mental Health Counseling</u>, <u>11</u>(4), 384-395.**

Developmental counseling approaches are recommended based on the results of this study, which suggest that aging has a positive affect on self-disclosure patterns. Older persons more readily self-disclose in counseling sessions than do younger persons.

2   **Ito, H., & Sato, S. (1986). Health promotion in Japan: An overview. <u>Health Promotion</u>, <u>1, 2</u>, 213-218.**

The article reviews health promotion in Japan from a historical perspective. The details of current health promotion activities are discussed, and recommendations are made for a more comprehensive national health promotion plan.

3   **Kinnier, R.T., & Metha, A.T. (1989). Regrets and priorities at three stages of life. <u>Counseling and Values</u>, <u>33</u>(3), 182-193.**

Subjects of different ages were surveyed concerning their major regrets and priorities in life. All subjects expressed regrets over missed educational opportunities, while older subjects rated family higher and expressed more regrets about not spending enough time with family members. The least satisfied subjects wished they had taken more risks in their lives.

4   **Smyer, M.A. (1984). Life transitions and aging: Implications for counseling older adults. <u>Counseling Psychologist</u>, <u>12</u>(2), 17-28.**

A conceptual framework for counseling older adults and their families is recommended. Counselors need to assist older clients in differentiating normal from abnormal aspects of aging and focus on preventive interventions with older persons and their families.

5   Teitelman, J., & Parham, I. (1990). Fundamentals of geriatrics for health professionals: An annotated bibliography. Westport, CT: Greenwood Press.

This book presents a compilation of references related to geriatrics for health professionals. An introduction provides an overview of the topic. This is followed by an extensive list of citations and brief annotations arranged by subject.

6   Toner, H.M., & Morris, J.D. (1992). A social-psychological perspective of dietary quality in later adulthood. Journal of Nutrition for the Elderly, 11(4), 35-53.

This study involved 100 community-dwelling elderly adults to determine if there was a relationship between self-actualization and social support, and one's dietary intake. The results indicated that one's dietary quality was positively influenced by one's internal motivation, and support from family and friends.

7   Yan, A. (1985). Dietary factors of frail elderly Chinese in community-based long-term care. Journal of Nutrition for the Elderly, 5(1), 37-46.

Alternative service delivery systems are required for members of various ethnic populations. Culturally adaptive food and seasoning are shown as essential to improving the acceptability of meals for older Chinese individuals.

DEMOGRAPHY OF AGING

8   Cavallaro, M. (1991). Curriculum guidelines and strategies on counseling older women for incorporation into gerontology and counseling coursework. Special Issue: Women, education, and aging. Educational Gerontology, 17(2), 157-166.

This article includes a discussion of several topics which should be incorporated into curriculum in gerontology and counseling. Topics which are discussed include health, physiological changes, osteoporosis, mental health, changes in family relationships, sexuality, substance abuse, and resources.

9   Duffy, M., & MacDonald, E. (1990). Determinants of functional health of older persons. Gerontologist, 30(4), 503-509.

This article reported the results of a study to investigate the relationships among demographics, self-esteem, health locus of control, health promotion, behaviors, perceived health, and functional health in older persons. Findings indicated that exercise and nutrition may increase scores on five functional dimensions. Implications for counseling are discussed.

10 Miller, B., & McFall, S. (1991). Stability and change in the informal task support network of frail older persons. Gerontologist, 31(6), 735-745.

The 1982 and 1984 national Long-Term Care Survey data and Informal Caregivers Survey was analyzed to determine predictors of stability and change in composition, size, and intensity of help of the informal task support networks of frail older persons and their primary caregivers. Findings included changes in the size and intensity of support networks related to decrease in health and functional status of the older person but no change in relation to increased caregiver burden. Race and relationship to caregiver were also predictors of size and intensity of network. Implications for practice are included.

11 Scharlach, A. (1989). A comparison of employed caregivers of cognitively impaired and physically impaired elderly persons. Research on Aging, 11(2), 225-243.

This article reports the results of a study investigating differences in caregiving among caregivers of cognitively impaired and physically impaired older persons. Higher levels of emotional, physical and financial strain were reported among caregivers of cognitively impaired elderly compared to caregivers of physically impaired older persons. Additionally, caregivers to cognitively impaired older persons were more likely to report that caregiving had a negative effect on their personal and work lives. Implication for practice are discussed.

12 Shenk, D. (1990). Aging in a changing ethnic context: The Lebanese-American family. Ethnic Groups, 8(3), 147-161.

Two models of the Lebanese-American family are studied to explore the needs of the elderly popultation and their families within the context of their culture. The changing role of the extended family network and the impact this has on service needs is also discussed.

ATTITUDES TOWARD OLDER PERSONS

13 Adelman, R. (1988). A well elderly program: An intergenerational model in medical evaluation. Gerontologist, 28(3), 409-413.

This article describes a model designed to dispel ageist attitudes and myths in medical students. Results indicate that exposing medical students to healthy elderly may positively impact attitudes.

14   Beaver, J.L. (1991). <u>Aged stereotypes and their effects on older persons' self-esteem</u>. (MF01/PC03). Ohio University, Masters Paper. (ERIC document Reproduction Service No. ED 334492)

This article conducts a literature review of stereotypes and attitudes about older persons, and the effects such stereotypes have upon the mental health of older persons. The article concludes that, in general, society projects negative images and attitudes about aging and older persons, and that these attitudes can have many negative effects on the aged.

15   Myers, J.E. (1990). <u>Empowerment for later life</u>. ERIC.

This text hypothesizes that American society unfairly and arbitrarily restricts the opportunities and activities of older persons based purely on their age. The text explores in detail the idea of empowering older persons to overcome the negative effects of societal attitudes by helping the aged gain a sense of power and control in their lives.

16   Ponzo, Z. (1981). Counseling the elderly: A lifetime process. <u>Counseling and Values</u>, <u>26</u>(1), 68-80.

This article focuses on the causes and effects of age prejudice. In particular, the article discusses the relationship between age prejudice and social changes.

PHYSIOLOGICAL ASPECTS OF AGING

17   Aman, M. (1990). Considerations in the use of psychotropic drugs in elderly mentally retarded persons. <u>Journal of Mental Deficiency Research</u>, <u>34</u>(1), 1-10.

This article reviews the pharmacokinetic variables which are associated with the use of psychotropic drugs in elderly mentally retarded persons. Factors which influence drugs actions in older persons are discussed. Implications and guidelines for use of psychotropic drugs with elderly mentally retarded persons are included.

18   Burgio, L., & Gurgio, K. (1986). Behavioral gerontology: Application of behavioral methods to the problems of older adults. <u>Journal of Applied Behavioral Analysis</u>, <u>19</u>(4), 321-328.

This article reviews the current state of areas within behavioral gerontology which require further research. Implications for application are discussed and modifications of therapy which may be necessitated by physiological changes of aging are included.

19   Butler, R.N., Oberlink, M., & Schechter, M.   (Eds.).   (1990).   The
      promise of productive aging: From biology to social policy.   New
      York: Springer Publishing Company.

This book reviews the aging process and implications of aging from biological
aspects to the development of social policy. Comprehensive resource.

20   Brabilla, F.   (1992).   Psychopathological aspects of neuroendocrine
      diseases: Possible parallels with the psychoendocrine aspects of
      normal aging.   Special Issue: Psychoneuroendocrinology of aging:
      The brain as a target organ of hormones. Psychoneuroendocrinology,
      17(4), 283-291.

This article discusses psychopathological aspects of neuroendocrine disease and
the possible parallels with the psychoendocrine aspects of normal aging. Possible
links are discussed.

21   Caradoc-Davies, T.H., & Dixon, G.S. (1991). Factor analysis of activites
      of daily living scores: Culturally determined versus vegetative com-
      ponents. Clinical Rehabilitation, 5(1), 41-45.

A factor analysis of activities of daily living showed that 2 factors fit the
descriptions of vegetative and cultural factors. The activities required for survival
which fit the descriptions of vegetative factors, could not be relearned by subjects
with impaired cognitive ability or frailty. More advanced activites such as
dressing were found to be culturally learned, and could be relearned by the
subjects.

22   Cavallaro, M.   (1991).   Curriculum guidelines and strategies on
      counseling older women for incorporation into gerontology and coun-
      seling coursework.   Special Issue: Women, education, and aging.
      Educational Gerontology, 17(2), 157-166.

This article includes a discussion of several topics which should be incorporated
into curriculum in gerontology and counseling. Topics which are discussed
include health, physiological changes, osteoporosis, mental health, changes in
family relationships, sexuality, substance abuse, and resources.

23   Fielo, S., & Rizzolo, M.   (1985).   The effects of age on pharmaco-
      kinetics. Geriatric Nursing, 6(6), 328-331.

This article discusses the effects of aging on pharmacokinetics. Particular
attention is given to physiological changes which may alter the effects of drugs
in older persons.

24   Gold, D.T., Bales, C.W., Lyles, K.W., & Drezner, M.K. (1989).
      Treatment of osteoporosis: The psychological impact of a medical
      education program on older patients. Journal of the American
      Geriatrics Society, 37(5), 417-422.

The authors report the results of a study of participants in an intensive therapeutic
program for osteoporosis over a one-year period. Various types of information
and counseling produced improved psychological outlooks in spite of persistent
and chronic pain.

25   Hoffman, A., Lieberman, S., & Ceda, G. (1992). Growth hormone
      therapy in the elderly: Implications for the aging brain. Special Issue:
      Psychoneuroendocrinology of aging: The brain as a target organ of
      hormones. Psychoneuroendocrinology, 17(4), 327-333.

This article includes a discussion of the possible effects of growth hormone on
various aspects of the normal aging process such as muscle atrophy and
osteoporosis. Research related to growth hormone and aging is reviewed.

26   Hussey, L. (1991). Overcoming the clinical barriers of low literacy
      and medication noncompliance among the elderly. Journal of
      Gerontological Nursing, 17(3), 27-29.

This article reviews the problems associated with medication compliance among
the elderly. Factors contributing to noncompliance and strategies to enhance
compliance are presented. Case example is included.

27   Jennings, R., Nebes, R., & Brock, K. (1988). Memory retrieval in
      noise and psychophysiological response in the young and old.
      Psychophysiology, 25(6), 633-644.

This article reports the results of a study investigating memory retrieval in noise
and psychophysiological responses in young and old individuals. Data from the
study is presented and implications of the results are included.

28   Mitrushina, M., Satz, P., Chervinsky, A., & D'Elia, L. (1991).
      Performance of four age groups of normal elderly on the Rey
      Auditory-Verbal Learning Test. Journal of Clinical Psychology, 47(3),
      351-357.

This article presents the results of a study investigating the effect of age on
encoding, retention, and retrieval aspects of memory in older persons. The Rey
Auditory-Verbal Learning Test was used. Results indicate that faculty retrieval
mechanisms were present and that encoding and retention processes were not
affected by aging. Implications are included.

29   Mooradian, A. (1988). Effect of aging on the blood-brain barrier. Neurobiology of Aging, 9(1), 31-39.

This article reviews the changes in the blood-brain barrier associated with aging and age related disease. Changes associated with Alzheimer's disease are highlighted.

30   Palmore, E. (1986). Trends in the health of the aged. Gerontologist, 26(3), 298-302.

This article utilizes a review of the data from the Health Interview Survey of the National Center for Health Statistics to assert that the relative health among the aged has improved substantially in the period 1961-1981. Explanations of this trend are included.

31   Reuben, D., Silliman, R., & Traines, M. (1988). The aging driver: Medicine, policy, and ethics. Journal of the American Geriatrics Society, 36(12), 1135-1142.

This article discusses the medical and ethical roles of the physician in regard to making decisions regarding aging drivers. Physiological changes and diseases associated with aging which may affect the older persons ability to drive are discussed. Implications for practice are included.

32   Teitelman, J., & Parham, I. (1990). Fundamentals of geriatrics for health professionals: An annotated bibliography. Westport, CT: Greenwood Press.

This book presents a compilation of references related to geriatrics for health professionals. An introduction provides an overview of the topic. This is followed by an extensive list of citations and brief annotations arranged by subject.

33   Whitnourne, S. (1990). Sexuality in the aging male. Generations, 14(3), 28-30.

This article presents an overview of the physiological and psychological changes associated with male sexuality and aging. Normal changes associated with aging as well as certain pathology which may affect sexuality are discussed. Implications for couples are also included.

PSYCHOLOGICAL ASPECTS OF AGING

34   Agresti, A. (1990). Cognitive screening of the older client. Journal of
       Mental Health Counseling, 12(3), 384-392.

This article outlines the purposes and goals of cognitive screening with older
clients. Common misconceptions regarding late-life cognitive functioning and the
necessity for thorough assessment are emphasized.

35   Brown, M.T. (1989). A cross-sectional analysis of self-disclosure
       patterns. Journal of Mental Health Counseling, 11(4), 384-395.

The responses to Jourard's Self-Disclosure Questionnaire from 30 men and 37
women were utilized to study the effects aging on self-disclosure. Aging was
found to have an effect on disclosure patterns.

36   Burgio, L., & Gurgio, K. (1986). Behavioral gerontology: Application
       of behavioral methods to the problems of older adults. Journal of
       Applied Behavioral Analysis, 19(4), 321-328.

This article reviews the current state of areas within behavioral gerontology
which require further research. Implications for application are discussed and
modifications of therapy which may be necessitated by physiological changes of
aging are included.

37   Butler, R., & Lewis, M. (1986). Aging and mental health: Positive
       psycho-social and biomedical approaches. In R. Butler (Ed.), Aging and
       mental health. Columbus, OH: Merrill.

This book chapter presents a discussion of positive psychosocial and biomedical
approaches which may be used by health professionals working with older
persons and their families. In addition this book represents an important resource
for health professionals concerned with issues of mental health and aging.

38   Cavallaro, M. (1991). Curriculum guidelines and strategies on
       counseling older women for incorporation into gerontology and
       counseling coursework. Special Issue: Women, education, and aging.
       Educational Gerontology, 17(2), 157-166.

This article includes a discussion of several topics which should be incorporated
into curriculum in gerontology and counseling. Topics which are discussed
include health, physiological changes, osteoporosis, mental health, changes in
family relationships, sexuality, substance abuse, and resources.

39   Crane, F.W., & Kramer, B.J. (1987). Perceptions of losses in the later
       years. Counseling and Values, 31(2), 185-159.

The perceptions of 447 service providers and 983 older adults relative to the seriousness of 21 losses were compared. Responses of the two groups differed significantly, suggesting that older adults become more proactive in their treatment programs and service providers re-examine the content of their pre- and in-service training programs.

40   Goldman, A., & Carroll, J. (1990). Educational intervention as an adjunct to treatment in erectile dysfunction in older couples. Journal of Sex and Marital Therapy, 16(3), 127-141.

This article reports the results of a program designed to address the needs of older couples experiencing erectile dysfunction. Information regarding psychological and physical changes of normal aging is included. Results included increased knowledge of the psychological and physical changes of aging and increased sexual satisfaction. Implications for use of educational intervention with this population are included.

41   Jennings, R., Nebes, R., & Brock, K. (1988). Memory retrieval in noise and psychophysiological response in the young and old. Psychophysiology, 25(6), 633-644.

This article reports the results of a study investigating memory retrieval in noise and psychophysiological responses in young and old individuals. Data from the study is presented and implications of the results are included.

42   Kellett, J. (1991). Sexuality of the elderly. Special Issue: Physical state and sexuality. Sexual and Marital Therapy, 6(2), 147-155.

This article presents a review of the literature regarding sexuality and aging. It is proposed that decreases in sexual activity with age are due largely to cultural and psychological factors rather than biological ability. Therefore, treatment interventions include information regarding normal psychological and physical changes associated with aging.

43   Mitrushina, M., Satz, P., Chervinsky, A., & D'Elia, L. (1991). Performance of four age groups of normal elderly on the Rey Auditory-Verbal Learning Test. Journal of Clinical Psychology, 47(3), 351-357.

This article presents the results of a study investigating the effect of age on encoding, retention, and retrieval aspects of memory in older persons. The Rey Auditory-Verbal Learning Test was used. Results indicate that faculty retrieval mechanisms were present and that encoding and retention processes were not affected by aging. Implications are included.

44   Palmore, E. (1985). How to live longer and like it. Sixth Annual Meeting of the Southern Gerontological Society. Journal of Applied Gerontology, 4(2), 1-8.

This article presents a review of the major predictors of longevity and life satisfaction related to the population of older persons. Emphasis is placed upon ways to live longer and to enjoy life more. Implications for practice are discussed.

45   Schonfield, D. (1989). Conflicting conclusions, gerontological theories and applications. Special Issue: Psychology of aging and gerontology. Canadian Psychology, 30(3), 507-515.

This article reviews the formulation of theories regarding psychological changes of aging. The development and construction of these theories needs to be based on a consensus of what age changes and differences are. The article emphasizes the need for agreement on these before constructing additional theories to answer complaints that the theoretical base is lacking.

46   Siegal, D. (1990). Women's reproductive changes: A marker, not a turning point. Generations, 14(3), 31-32.

This article reviews the psychological and physical changes associated with menopause. Conceptualizations of menopause and social issues are included. Implications for women in society are stressed.

47   Teitelman, J., & Parham, I. (1990). Fundamentals of geriatrics for health professionals: An annotated bibliography. Westport, CT: Greenwood Press.

This book presents a compilation of references related to geriatrics for health professionals. An introduction provides an overview of the topic. This is followed by an extensive list of citations and brief annotations arranged by subject.

SOCIAL ASPECTS OF AGING

48   Atchley, R.C. (1992). What do social theories of aging offer counselors? Counseling Psychologist, 20(2), 336-340.

This article is a response to an earlier 1992 article by Fry which discussed various social theories on aging. The Atchley article criticizes Fry for including discredited theories and omitting other more favored theories such as social breakdown theory.

49   Crose, R. (1992). Gerontology is only aging, it's not dead yet! <u>Counseling Psychologist</u>, <u>20</u>(2), 330-335.

This article is a response to an earlier 1992 article by Fry which discussed various social theories on aging. Although the article hails Fry's discussion of gerontological literature, it critiques Fry's presentation of working with older individuals as stereotypical.

50   Fry, P.S. (1992). Major social theories of aging and their implications for counseling concepts and practice: A critical review. <u>Counseling Psychologist</u>, <u>20</u>(2), 246-329.

This article explores various social theories on aging and their implication on counseling the aged. The primary focus of the article is on counseling theories designed to help the aged attain and maintain good mental health.

51   Monk, A. (1987). The "new" and the "young" aged. <u>Journal of Aging and Judaism</u>, <u>1, 2</u>, 146-165.

This article explores the meaning of terms such as "young" old, "new" aged, and "well" aged with respect to the population of Jewish elderly. In exploring the effects of rapid technological and cultural changes on the elderly, the article argues that continual, lifelong education is required for the aged to effectively cope with such changes.

52   Palmore, E. (1989). Social gerontology: An essential part of the "backbone." <u>Gerontology and Geriatrics Education</u>, <u>9</u>(4), 27-45.

This article outlines the important issues which need to be covered in a course in social gerontology. The importance of these topics in forming the "backbone of gerontology" is emphasized.

53   Qualls, S.H. (1992). Social gerontology theory is not enough: Strategies and resources for counselors. <u>Counseling Psychologist</u>, <u>20</u>(2), 341-345.

This article is a response to an earlier 1992 article by Fry which discussed various social theories on aging. The instant article, which is primarily laudatory of the Fry piece, adds to some of the central themes of Fry's article and cites additional references for counselors working with the elderly.

HEALTH AND WELLNESS IN LATER LIFE

54   Albert, M. (1987). Health screening to promote health for the elderly. <u>Nurse Practitioner: American Journal of Primary Health Care</u>, <u>12</u>(5).

This article discusses the advantages and difficulties inherent in health-screening with respect to the elderly. The article proposes a collection of screening strategies and techniques which can be used with the elderly and discusses various counseling techniques for reducing health risks in the elderly population.

55   Dickel, C.T. (1990, March). <u>Preserving elder autonomy: Moral and ethical considerations</u>. Paper presented at the Annual Convention of the American Association for Counseling and Development, Cincinnati, OH.

This article discusses in detail the importance of personal autonomy and the various ways in which the elderly lose freedom of choice with respect to their own lives. The article admonishes counselors to be aware of autonomy issues when counseling the elderly and to constantly seek what is best for their older patients.

56   Gioella, E.C. (1983). Healthy aging through knowledge and self-care. <u>Prevention in Human Services</u>, <u>3</u>(1), 39-51.

This article discusses the potentially health compromising physical and psychosocial changes that normally accompany the aging process. The article explains that various self-care activities, human services, and educational programs are needed to minimize the impact of the physical and psychosocial changes that accompany aging on the elderly.

57   Kligman, E.W. (1992). Preventive geriatrics: basic principles for primary care physicians. <u>Geriatrics</u>, <u>47</u>(7), 39-50.

This article discusses some of the barriers which impede the effectiveness of preventive geriatrics. The article also discusses in particular, the U.S. Prevention Services Task Force's proposed preventive geriatrics program.

58   McConatha, J.T., & McConatha, P.D. (1988-89). The study of the relationship between wellness and life satisfaction of older adults. <u>Activities, Adaptation and Aging</u>, <u>13</u>(1-2), 129-140.

This article examines the results of a survey of 167 adults 60 years or older to determine whether a relationship between life satisfaction and wellness exists. The article finds such a relationship and suggests that skills for maintaining wellness can be learned by the elderly.

59   McCormick, W.C., & Inui, T.S. (1992). Geriatric preventive care: Counseling techniques in practice settings. <u>Clinical Geriatric Medicine</u>, <u>8</u>(1), 215-228.

This article suggests that clinicians may encounter more difficulty in counseling patients with respect to preventive medicine than with managing acute illness. The article argues that communication difficulties between physicians, patients, and families of patients is a factor contributing to this state of affairs.

60   Ponzo, Z. (1992) Promoting successful aging: Problems, opportunities, and counseling guidelines. <u>Journal of Counseling and Development</u>, <u>71</u>(2), 210-213.

The article focuses on the promotion of healthy aging by encouraging counselors to become more involved in helping individuals and society to age more successfully. In addition, the article provides an overview of the problems, opportunities, and guidelines related to promoting successful aging which may benefit both the individual and society.

61   Toner, H.M., & Morris, J.D. (1992). A social-psychological perspective of dietary quality in later adulthood. <u>Journal of Nutrition for the Elderly</u>, <u>11</u>(4), 35-53.

This study involved 100 community-dwelling elderly adults to determine if there was a relationship between self-actualization and social support, and one's dietary intake. The results indicated that one's dietary quality was positively influenced by one's internal motivation, and support from family and friends.

62   Tucker, K.L., Dallal G.E., & Rush, D. (1992). Dietary patterns of elderly Boston-area residents defined by cluster analysis. <u>Journal of the American Dietetic Association</u>, <u>92</u>(12), 1487-1491.

Cluster analyis was utilized to determine common themes among the dietary patterns of 680 noninstitutionalized elderly volunteers. The study identified four significant patterns and made suggestions on ways to improve nutritional status based on these findings.

63   Wolfe, S.C., & Schirm, V. (1992). Medication counseling for the elderly: Effects on knowledge and compliance after hospital discharge. <u>Geriatric Nursing New York</u>, <u>13</u>(3), 134-138.

This study reports both qualitative and quantitative data which add to the nurse's understanding of medication knowledge and compliance in the elderly population. As elderly patients continue to assume more responsibility for self-care, it is essential for healthcare professionals to explore strategies for promoting self-care skills and well-being in this population.

64   Woolf, S.H., Kamerow, D.B., Lawrence, R.S., & Medalie, J.H. (1990). The periodic health examination of older adults: The recommendations of the U.S. preventive Services Task Force. <u>Journal of the American Geriatrics Society</u>, <u>38</u>(7), 817-823.

This article summarizes the recommendations for primary health prevention that should be included in periodic health examinations of older adults. Information and counseling are recommended for a variety of concerns.

65   Zumwalt, S.A., & Schmidt, R.M. (1989). The role of nutrition in AIDS and aging. Generations, 13(4), 77-79.

This article discusses the importance of the role of immunity for elderly patients and patient's with acquired immune deficiency syndrome. Additionally, the role of nutrition and counseling are discussed as methods to improve immune status.

SPIRITUALITY AND AGING

66   Becker, A.H. (1986). Pastoral theological implications of the aging process. Journal of Religion and Aging, 2(3), 13-30.

Life review is recommended as a way of enhancing development in later life which pastoral ministers can use to address the spiritual needs of older clients.

67   Bryant, M.D. (1989). Re-orienting pastoral care with aging persons. Journal of Religion and Aging, 5(3), 1-16.

In response to the special needs of the elderly population, this article recommends several ways for the church to re-focus pastoral care. The author discusses aging as a dynamic process, as well as the importance of theory and a systems approach.

68   DeMarinis, V. (1989). Spiritual, psychological, and social dimensions of pastoral care with patients and families in the home health care context. Pastoral Psychology, 37(4), 275-296.

This article examines the nature, function, and place of pastoral care in home health care. Training for clergy, especially in counseling, is addressed.

69   Klick, A.W., Ladrigan, P.M., & Fenity, N.D. (1987). Clergy request linkages: Implications for planning ministry with older adults. Educational Gerontology, 13(5), 437-442.

Clergy were surveyed to determine their training needs. Counseling received a high priority, however, there was a low need to clarify perceived attitudes about aging.

70   McCabe, S.P. (1985, August). Religion and aging. Paper presented at the Annual Convention of the American Psychological Association, Los Angeles, CA.

The lack of attention the elderly population has received from counseling psychology is discussed in this article which reviews the life transitions which may impact older persons. Religion is presented as a framework for understanding one's life pattern and present situation, as a strategy for coping with life transitions, as a source of goals which older persons can continue to move toward, and as a source of supportive social networking.

71   Schwanke, E.R. (1986). Providing pastoral care for the elderly in long term care facilities without a chaplain utilizing coordinated congregational resources. Journal of Religion and Aging, 2(3), 57-64.

Twelve church congregations worked together to provide spiritual care in six nursing homes which did not have chaplains. Meaningful visits were made by trained and supervised lay persons as well as trained chaplains.

72   Simmons, H., & Pierce, V. (1992). Pastoral responses to older adults and their families: An annotated bibliography. Westport, CT: Greenwood Press.

This book presents a compilation of references related to pastoral interventions with older adults and their families. An introduction provides an overview of the topic. This is followed by an extensive list of citations and brief annotations arranged by subject.

73   Uhlman, J., & Steinke, P.D. (1984). Pastoral visitation to the institutionalized aged: Delivering more than a lick and a promise. Pastoral Psychology, 32(4), 231-238.

This article describes a nationwide study of older persons in nursing homes conducted by the Lutheran Council USA. Older persons did not feel their needs were met in terms of time spent with them by chaplains. Older persons who had few visitors were most vulnerable.

AGING AND THE FAMILY

74   Cavallaro, M. (1991). Curriculum guidelines and strategies on counseling older women for incorporation into gerontology and counseling coursework. Special Issue: Women, education, and aging. Educational Gerontology, 17(2), 157-166.

This article includes a discussion of several topics which should be incorporated into curriculum in gerontology and counseling. Topics which are discussed include health, physiological changes, osteoporosis, mental health, changes in family relationships, sexuality, substance abuse, and resources.

75   Coyle, J. (1991). Families and aging: A selected, annotated bibliography. Westport, CT: Greenwood Press.

This book presents a compilation of references related to the topic of families and aging. An introduction provides an overview of the topic. This is followed by citations and brief annotations arranged by subject.

76   Eisenberg, D., & Carrilio, T.   (1990).   Friends of the family: Counseling elders at family service agencies.   Special Issue: Counseling and therapy for elders. Generations, 14(1), 25-26.

Family service agencies are discussed in terms of service to older persons in the community. The advantages and disadvantages of these services are discussed and specific issues for working with older persons included.

77   Erlanger, M.   (1990).   Using the genogram with the older client. Special Issue: Techniques for counseling older persons. Journal of Mental Health Counseling, 12(3), 321-331.

This article reviews the literature which suggests the usefulness of genogram for counseling older persons. The genogram allows the therapist to gain information on family relationships over several generations and may help to identify themes or factors important to the client. The therapeutic benefits of this approach are stressed and a case study is provided as a means of illustration.

78   Hansing, L.   (1986).   A program for the emotionally disturbed. Geriatric Nursing, 7(3), 137-139.

This article reports of the outcomes of three treatment programs for older persons established by a hospital in Minneapolis, MN. The three treatment program are described in detail and together they are presented as a comprehensive physiatric care program to older residents in the community.

79   Healey, C.B. (1987, April). Linking intergenerational need, knowledge, and service. Paper presented at the Annual Meeting of the Southern Gerontological Society, New Orleans, LA.

This paper reports the results of a study which was conducted to evaluate the LINKS (Linking Intergenerational Needs, Knowledge, and Services) project which was implemented to educational information, counseling, and information on existing resources to callers regarding older adults. Findings of earlier studies on the relationship of older persons and their families and the concern over the provision of affordable in-home care for older persons were confirmed.

80   Hinkle, S.   (1990).   An overview of dementia in older persons: Identification, diagnosis, assessment, and treatment.   Special Issue: Techniques for counseling older persons. Journal of Mental Health Counseling, 12(3), 368-383.

This article describes the clinical aspects of dementia, assessment, diagnostic criteria, and interventions for use with demented older persons.   Family intervention is included among the recommended treatment modalities. Additionally, individual counseling, support groups, and medication therapy are recommended. Emphasis is on clinical intervention.

81   Morse, R. (1989). Roles of the psychotherapist in family financial counseling: A systems approach to prolongation of independence. Journal of Psychotherapy and the Family, 5(1-2), 133-147.

This article takes a holistic approach to psychotherapy with older persons and proposes that therapists can assist clients in the integration of good health, self-worth, and a sense of economic security. Steps for developing a financial analysis with older persons are provided and the implications for practice discussed.

82   Reuben, D., Silliman, R., & Traines, M. (1988). The aging driver: Medicine, policy, and ethics. Journal of the American Geriatrics Society, 36(12), 1135-1142.

This article discusses the medical and ethical roles of the physician in regard to making decisions regarding aging drivers. Physiological changes and diseases associated with aging which may affect the older persons ability to drive are discussed. Implications for practice are included.

83   Scharlach, A.E. (1985, November). Treating the aging family: Demystifying dysfunctional role expectations. Paper presented at the Annual Scientific Meeting of the Gerontological Society, New Orleans, LA.

Problems experienced by families with aging members are discussed in terms of family role expectations and dysfunctional societal attitudes and beliefs that make family conflict inevitable with regard to family roles. A treatment model which includes clarification of role expectations, promotion of personal autonomy, and enhancement of relationship quality is presented to relieve strain associated with such dysfunctional beliefs.

84   Schwartzben, S. (1989). The 10th floor family support group: A descriptive model of the use of a multi-family group in a home for the aged. Special Issue: Social work with multi-family groups. Social Work with Groups, 12(1), 41-54.

This article describes a multi-family group experience in an institutional setting. The role of the social worker is discussed and emphasized. Strengths of the program are included as well as implications for clinical practice.

2

Older Persons with Impairments

85 Balmer, D.H. (1989). The CARE Project: The evaluation of group counseling as a therapeutic intervention for patients with rheumatoid arthritis. British Journal of Guidance and Counselling, 17(3), 304-316.

This article reports the results of a study of counseling services provided as part of the Counselling and Arthritis Research Evaluation project. Although qualitative analyses showed that counseling was therapeutic, quantitative results showed that it made no difference.

86 Bourland, G., & Lundervold, D.A. (1989). Acceptability ratings for interventions on problematic behavior of older adults. Journal of Clinical and Experimental Gerontology, 11(3-4), 105-113.

Low income older persons serving as foster grandparents in an institution for persons with developmental disabilities were surveyed as to preferences for interventions to deal with problematic behaviors. They expressed a preference for counseling as opposed to time outs or restraints.

87 Brown, R., & Hughson, E.A. (1989). Towards a model of rehabilitation. International Journal for the Advancement of Counseling, 12(1), 29-38.

An integration of behavioral methods is recommended for helping persons with a wide range of disabling conditions, including disabilities relating to aging. Empowerment and consumer control are important strategies with all disabled populations.

88 Butler, R.N. (1984). Senile dementia: Reversible and irreversible. Counseling Psychologist, 12(2), 75-79.

Some of the normal mental changes that accompany aging may be misperceived as a result of myths surrounding the process of senility. Treatment based on environmental modifications for reversible and irreversible dementias are discussed.

89   Decker, T.W., Cline-Elsen, J., & Gallagher, M. (1992). Relaxation therapy as an adjunct in radiation oncology. Journal of Clinical Psychology, 48(3), 388-393.

This article presents the results of a study which examined the impact of education and counseling the stress, anxiety, and depression cancer patients may experience while undergoing palliative and curative radiation therapy. In a pre-test/post-test study using the Profile of Mood States significant reductions were found in tension, depression, anger, and fatigue.

90   Dracup, K., Meleis, A.I., Clark, S., Clyburn, A., Shields, L., & Staley, M. (1984). Group counseling in cardiac rehabilitation: effect on patient compliance. Patient Education and Counseling, 6(4), 169-177.

This study examines the effects of group counseling as a strategy for increasing patient compliance in a cardiac patient population.

91   Emery, C.F., Leatherman, N.E., Burker, E.J., & MacIntyre, N.R. (1991). Psychological outcomes of a pulmonary rehabilitation program. Chest: The Cardiopulmonary Journal, 100(3), 613-617.

This article discusses the psychological outcomes of a pulmonary rehabilitation program.

92   Evans, R.L. (1986). Cognitive telephone group therapy with physically disabled elderly persons. Gerontologist, 26(1), 8-11.

The author studied the effectiveness of a cognitive group therapy by telephone counseling program for severely disabled older persons. Most of the participants reported decreased feelings of loneliness.

93   Frey, J., Swanson, G.S., & Hyer, L. (1989). Strategic interventions for chronic patients in later life. American Journal of Family Therapy, 17(1), 27-33.

This article presents a systems approach to treatment of older persons with chronic psychiatric problems. A case example with an older couple is provided.

94   Gold, D.T., Bales, C.W., Lyles, K.W., & Drezner, M.K. (1989). Treatment of osteoporosis: The psychological impact of a medical education program on older patients. Journal of the American Geriatrics Society, 37(5), 417-422.

The authors report the results of a study of participants in an intensive therapeutic program for osteoporosis over a one-year period. Various types of information and counseling produced improved psychological outlooks in spite of persistent and chronic pain.

95   Kersten, L. (1990). Changes in self-concept during pulmonary rehabilitation part 2. Heart and Lung: Journal of Critical Care, 19(5 part 1), 463-470.

This study utilizes a 20-item semantic meaning differential scale to measure the effects of counseling on patient self-esteem while participating in a multidisciplinary pulmonary rehabilitation program. Findings from this study establish the utility of this Self-concept Evaluation tool in adult patients.

96   Ross, A.M., Pitts, L.H., & Kobayashi, S. (1992). Prognosticators of outcome after major head injury in the elderly. Journal of Neuroscience and Nursing, 24(2), 88-93.

The findings of this study have implications for nurses and other health professionals counseling patients and families following major head injuries.

97   Schover, L.R. (1993). Sexual rehabilitation after treatment for prostate cancer. Cancer, 71(3 Suppl), 1024-1030.

This article indicates the need for counseling of the patient and sexual partners as part of the rehabilitation process in patients receiving treatments for prostate cancer.

98   Tresch, D.D., Sims, F.H., & Edmund, H. (1991). Patients in a persistent vegetative state: Attitudes and reactions of family members. Journal of the American Geriatrics Society, 39(1), 17-21.

This study examined the attitudes and reactions of family members to patients in persistent vegetative states. Most family members were committed to the survival of the patient and indicated desires for counseling.

99   Tueth, M.J. (1993). Anxiety in the older patient: differential diagnosis and treatment. Geriatrics, 48(2), 51-54.

This article discusses the importance of differentiating anxiety in the older client as a symptom of an underlying mental or physical disorder versus a primary diagnosis. Additionally, the article explores treatment strategies.

PHYSICALLY DISABLED OLDER PERSONS

100   Abrams, H.B., Hnath, C.T., Guerreiro, S.M., & Ritterman, S.I. (1992). The effects of intervention strategy on self-perception of hearing handicap. Ear Hear, 13(5), 371-377.

In this study, the Hearing Handicap Inventory for the Elderly was used to measure the effects of counseling in combination with hearing aid use in aural rehabilitation. Results indicated that counseling in combination with hearing aid use resulted in a greater reduction of self-perceived hearing handicap than did use of a hearing aid alone or no intervention.

101   Bowman, G. (1992). Using therapeutic metaphor in adjustment counseling. Journal of Visual Impairment and Blindness, 86(10), 440-442.

In this article, the author explores the design and therapeutic use of metaphor in counseling persons who are blind. In addition, the author includes examples of metaphorical studies developed through his work as a rehabilitation teacher.

102   Finnerty-Fried, P. (1985). Adapting rehabilitation counseling for older persons. Rehabilitation Counseling Bulletin, 29(2), 135-142.

Social, psychological and physiological changes related to the aging process are outlined. The author proposes adaptations for rehabilitation practitioners working with older clients.

103   Goffinet, J.M. (1992). Hearing loss and hearing aid use by the elderly: A primer for the geriatric care professional. Educational Gerontology, 18(3), 257-264.

Older persons commonly deny the existence of hearing problems, often because of the stigma of such problems as related to aging. Rehabilitative approaches which are most effective will include screening, medical treatment, counseling, and use of hearing aids and assistive devices.

104   Hittner, A., & Bornstein, H. (1990). Group counseling with older adults: Coping with late-onset hearing impairment. Journal of Mental Health Counseling, 12(3), 332-341.

Counselors working with older adults should expect that 25% of their clients will experience hearing difficulties. Suggestions for modifying group counseling interventions to accommodate the needs of older hearing impaired clients are provided.

105   Jinks, M.J. (1991). Counseling older adults with hearing impairment. Journal of Practical Nursing, 41(3), 43-51.

This article explores the issues involved in counseling older adults with hearing impairment.

106   Kaplan, H. (1988). Communication problems of the hearing impaired elderly: What can be done? Pride Institute Journal of Long Term Home Health Care, 7(1), 10-22.

This article describes the types of hearing loss that older persons experience and the treatments which are available. The goals of aural rehabilitation and the importance of informational counseling for older persons and their families are stressed.

107   Nosek, M.A., Fuhrer, M.J., & Hughes, S.O. (1991). Perceived counselor credibility by persons with physical disability: Influence of counselor status, professional status, and the counseling content. Rehabilitation Psychology, 36(3), 153-161.

This study explored the influence of counselor status, professional status, and counseling content on perceived counselor credibility by persons with physical disability. Results indicated that counselors with disabilities were rated more favorably than counselors without disabilities. This preference was found to be particularly prevalent when the counseling content was disability related and when the counselors were presented as nonprofessionals.

108   Timmerman, S. (1987-88). Learning to overcome disability. Generations, 12(2), 46-48.

A program of education and counseling is presented as an effective means of helping older persons increase independent living and self-reliance. This program emphasizes one-to-one counseling and instruction.

DEVELOPMENTALLY DISABLED OLDER PERSONS

109   Aman, M. (1990). Considerations in the use of psychotropic drugs in elderly mentally retarded persons. Journal of Mental Deficiency Research, 34(1), 1-10.

This article reviews the pharmacokinetic variables which are associated with the use of psychotropic drugs in elderly mentally retarded persons. Factors which influence drugs actions in older persons are discussed. Implications and guidelines for use of psychotropic drugs with elderly mentally retarded persons are included.

110   Caserta, M.S., Connelly, J.R., Lund, D.E., & Poulton, J.L. (1987).
       Older adult caregivers of developmentally disabled household
       members: Service needs and fulfillment. Journal of Gerontological
       Social Work, 10(1-2), 35-50.

This article reports the results of a study which examined the service needs and
level of fulfillment for older adult caregivers of developmentally disabled
household members. Information was obtained using indepth, in-home interviews.
Results indicated a significant need for key services including housekeeping,
home repairs, personal counseling, legal services, and medical doctor services.
Implications for future interventions and policy are included.

111   Edelson, R. (1990). ARTS AND CRAFTS - not "arts and crafts":
       Alternative vocational day activities for adults who are older and
       mentally retarded. Special Issue: Activities with developmentally
       disabled elderly and older adults. Activities, Adaptation, and Aging,
       15(1-2), 81-97.

This article describes a program in which developmentally disabled and retarded
older persons participated in an vocational day activity program where they sold
art and fine handwork which they had produced. The implications of aging and
developmental disabilities on self-esteem were also discussed and the program
presented as a way to enhance self-concept.

112   Gibson, J., Rabkin, J., & Munson, R. (1992). Critical issues in serving
       the developmentally disabled elderly. Journal of Gerontological Social
       Work, 19(1), 35-49.

This article presents the findings of a qualitative research study which
interviewed 29 key informants regarding developmentally disabled older persons
and aging service networks. Results included the identification of critical issues
related to this population. They were normative aging and health care, access to
community-based programs and services, and the need for service providers to
work with family caregivers and advocates. Training needs for service providers
was also surveyed and reported. Implications for training and practice are
discussed.

113   McDaniel, B.A. (1989). A group work experience with mentally
       retarded adults on the issues of death and dying. Journal of
       Gerontological Social Work, 13(3-4), 187-191.

A support group for eight older adults with mild mental retardation is described.
The group focused on death and dying, with positive benefits for participants.

114 Smith, G.C., & Tobin, S.S. (1989, November). <u>How case managers</u> <u>perceive older parents as caregivers of developmentally disabled adult</u> <u>offsprings</u>. Paper presented at the Annual Scientific Meeting of the Gerontological Society, Minneapolis, MN.

This article presents the results of pilot study including ll intensive interviews with case managers about their work with parents of developmentally disabled adults. Results indicate several issues related to aging parents as caregivers of their developmentally disabled adult children. Additionally, results indicate the need for geriatric specialists to serve both aging developmentally disabled clients and their elderly caregivers.

115 Tedrick, T. (1990). Aging, developmental disabilities and leisure: Policy and service delivery issues. Special Issue: Activities with developmentally disabled elderly and older adults. <u>Activities,</u> <u>Adaptation, and Aging,</u> 15(1-2), 141-152.

This article reviews the challenges faced by the aging network and staff serving older persons who are developmentally disabled and/or mentally retarded. As this population begins to live longer, aging programs must provide services designed to meet the special needs of this group. Implications for legislation, policy, and practice are discussed.

116 Wilhite, B., Keller, M., & Nicholson, L. (1990). Integrating older persons with developmental disabilities into community recreation: Theory to practice. Special Issue: Activities with developmentally disabled elderly and older adults. <u>Activities, Adaptation, and Aging,</u> 15(1-2), 111-129.

This article details an 8-step model for integrating developmentally disabled elders and their non-disabled counterparts. The importance of providing recreational activities for both groups as well as opportunities for empowerment are stressed. A case study is included for illustration of the model.

117 Zimple, B. (1990). Sharing activities: The Onedia County A.R.C. Cornhill Senior Center Integration Project. Special Issue: Activities with developmentally disabled elderly and older adults. <u>Activities,</u> <u>Adaptation, and Aging,</u> 15(1-2), 131-139.

This article describes a program in which developmentally disabled elderly and older adults were involved in an integrated program with non-disabled peers. Friendships and socialization developed between the groups. Implications for practice are included.

CHRONIC AND ACUTE ILLNESSES

118   Burgener, S., & Logan, G. (1989). Sexuality concerns of the post-stroke patient. Rehabilitation Nursing, 14(4), 178-181.

This article reviews the research related to sexuality in the post-stroke patient and research findings are related to important issues for healthcare providers to consider in rehabilitation of post-stroke patients.

119   Crenshaw, T.L. (1986). Dyspareunia due to senile vaginitis and vaginal atrophy. Medical Aspects of Human Sexuality, 20(9), 22-28.

The case of a 64 year old woman with severe dyspareunia is described. Following medical treatment, estrogen replacement, and counseling, she resumed sexual activity after eight years of abstinence.

120   D'Eramo-Melkus, G.A., Wylie-Rosett, J., & Hagan, J.A. (1992). Metabolic impact of education in NIDDM. Diabetes Care, 15(7), 864-869.

This study was designed to evaluate the impact of a model of diabetes education and weight reduction on diabetes control and weight loss in obese individuals with non-insulin-dependent diabetes mellitus. The results of the study have implications for counselors. These include the findings which indicate that a cognitive behavioral group intervention which includes diabetes knowledge and weight reduction training can produce improvements in diabetes control while there appears to be no advantage to the additional of individual counseling as a follow-up maintenance strategy.

121   Decker, T.W., Cline-Elsen, J., & Gallagher, M. (1992). Relaxation therapy as an adjunct in radiation oncology. Journal of Clinical Psychology, 48(3), 388-393.

The results of a study designed to examine the impact of relaxation therapy, including relaxation training and imagery, on patients undergoing curative and palliative radiotherapy are reported. Results indicate significant reductions in the treatment group in tension, depression, anger,and fatigue. Based on these findings, the study concludes that relaxation therapy appears to improve psychological well-being and quality of life in these patients.

122   Denollet, J. (1993). Emotional distress and fatigue in coronary heart disease: the Global Mood Scale (GMS). Psychological Medicine, 23(1), 111-121.

This study was designed to devise and test a psychometrically sound and practical measure of emotional distress in patients with coronary heart disease. Findings indicate the Global Mood Scale is both theoretically and psychometrically sound as a measure of emotional distress in patients with coronary heart disease. Additionally, the Global Mood Scale was found to be sufficiently sensitive to assess change in emotional distress.

123 Finn, H., Schenee, J., Klein, I., & Rimmerman, A. (1990). The rehabilitation of people suffering from chronic psychoses: The N.Y.P.C.C. study. Revista-de-Psiquiatria-de-la-Facultad-de-Medicina-de-Barcelona, Special Education, 30-33.

This study was designed to examine the effects of a rehabilitation program designed to meet the needs of people suffering from chronic psychoses residing in three adult homes in New York. The results of a questionnaire designed by the New York Psychotherapy and Counseling Center suggest that the provision of psychosocial rehabilitation services may result in progress in areas such as symptomatology, social interaction activities, and therapeutic goals. Progress was most likely to occur when individual and group counseling is provided in combination with medical treatment.

124 Gonzalez, S., Steinglass, P., & Reiss, D. (1989). Putting the illness in its place: Discussion groups for families with chronic medical illnesses. Family Process, 28(1), 63-87.

The authors describe a new psychosocial intervention for families and patients experiencing the chronic phases of disabling illnesses. A short-term, highly structured, psychoeducationally oriented, multiple family discussion group was successful with a wide range of disabling conditions.

125 Hellman, C.J., Budd, M., Borysenko, J., & McClelland, D.C. (1990). A study of the effectiveness of two group behavioral medicine interventions for patients with psychosomatic complaints. Behavioral Medicine, 16(4), 165-173.

This study compared the effectiveness of behavioral interventions and information about stress management and the relationship of stress and illness. Behavioral strategies were more effective for persons of all ages in decreasing physical and psychological discomfort.

126 Kirschenbaum, D.S., Sherman, J., & Penrod, J.D. (1987). Promoting self-directed hemodialysis: Measurement and cognitive-behavioral intervention. Health Psychology, 6(5), 373-385.

Four older patients participated in a study in which behavioral observations and treatment of hemodialysis resulted in a higher level of self-care. Decisional counseling, behavior contracting, self-monitoring, and staff-monitoring were components of the program.

127 McCarthy, B., Kuipers, L., Hurry, J., & Harper, R. (1989). Counseling the relatives of the long-term mentally ill: A low cost supportive model. British Journal of Psychiatry, 154, 775-782.

This article describes a counseling and support group which was implemented for relatives of older persons seen in adult day care programs. The intervention was effective in helping to alleviate emotional reactions to caregiving.

128 Moss, R.J., Mastri, A.R., & Schut, L.J. (1988). The coexistence and differentiation of late onset Huntington's disease and Alzheimer's disease: A case report and review of the literature.

The authors recommend genetic counseling for families in which Huntington's Disease has been diagnosed, based on a complicated case presentation of an individual with both Huntington's and Alzheimer's Disease.

129 Relf, M.V. (1991). Sexuality and the older bypass patient. Geriatric Nursing: American Journal of Care for the Aging, 12(6), 294-296.

This article discusses nursing implications associated with issues surrounding sexuality and the older bypass patient.

130 Riensche, L.L., & Lang, K. (1992). Treatment of swallowing disorders through a multidisciplinary team approach. Educational Gerontology, 18(3), 277-284.

Disordered swallowing commonly occurs with many age-related disorders and can contribute to a fear of eating. Because social, psychological, medical, and economic consequences may occur, a multidisciplinary approach to treatment is recommended.

131 Russell, N.K., & Roter, D.L. (1993). Health promotion counseling of chronic-disease patients during primary care visits. American Journal of Public Health, 83(7), 979-982.

This study examined patient-physician interaction and health promotion counseling. Results indicate that physicians spent nearly 60% of the discussion during primary care visits with chronic disease patients attempting encourage behavior change using behavioral counseling techniques. Strategies for improving physician effectiveness are discussed.

TERMINAL ILLNESS

132 Allers, C.T. (1990). AIDS and the older adult. Gerontologist, 30(3), 405-407.

This article describes the roles, issues, and conflicts which older adults face when relatives or neighbors are diagnosed with AIDS. The need for counseling and support for older caregivers is stressed.

133 Charlton, R. (1992). Palliative care in non-cancer patients and the neglected caregiver. Journal of Clinical Epidemiology, 45(12), 1447-1449.

This article discusses the implications of palliative care for non-cancer patients. Case studies are included.

134 Lloyd, G.A. (1989). AIDS & Elders: Advocacy, activism, & coalitions. Generations, 13(4), 32-35.

This article proposes that based upon many shared policy and discrimination issues, advocates for persons with AIDS and advocates for older persons might be expected to form a natural coalition. However, given that both groups will be competing for the same resources in a time of human service program reductions, this coalition seems unlikely.

135 Payne, S. (1989). Anxiety and depression in women with advanced cancer: Implications for counselling. Counselling Psychology Quarterly, 2(3), 337-344.

This study determined that levels of anxiety and depression were lower among cancer patients treated at home than among those treated in the hospital.

136 Tchekmedyian, N.S., Zahyna, D., Halpert, C., & Heber, D. (1992). Assessment and maintenance of nutrition in older cancer patients. Oncology-Hunting, 6(2 Suppl), 105-111.

This study discusses the assessment and maintenance of nutrition and quality of life in older cancer patients. Ongoing support and education, food supplementation, and attention to activity level are important to the maintenance of quality of life and nutritional status in these patients.

ALZHEIMER'S DISEASE

137 Hinkle, S. (1990). An overview of dementia in older persons: Identification, diagnosis, assessment, and treatment. Journal of Mental Health Counseling, 12(3), 368-383.

This article describes the clinical aspects of dementia and examines diagnostic criteria, assessment techniques, and recommendations for treatment in older clients. Individual and family interventions are recommended, as well as support groups and medication therapy.

138   Kirwin, P.M. (1985-86). Adult day care: An integrated model. Journal of Gerontological Social Work, 9(2), 59-71.

Integrating adult day care and senior center programs increases participant options while decreasing service cost, and is recommended in planning community service options for frail elderly individuals.

139   LaBarge, E., Rosenman, L.S., Leavitt, K., & Cristiani, T. (1988). Counseling clients with mild senile dementia of the Alzheimer's type: A pilot study. Journal of Neurologic Rehabilitation, 2(4), 167-173.

Clients with mild senile dementia were administered cognitive psychometric measures, then seen in a follow up counseling session for test interpretation and supportive counseling. The subjects developed helpful attitudes, used coping mechanisms, and identified strengths to compensate for their memory losses.

DEPRESSION

140   Burlingame, V.S. (1988). Counseling an older person. Social Casework, 69(9), 588-592.

A case study of an 84 year old depressed woman is presented. Diagnosis and treatment were developed through home visits, clinic interviews, psychiatric evaluation, and group therapy.

141   Garratt, J.P. (1992). Depression in the elderly. Physician Assistant, 16(3), 101-104, 110, 112.

This article provides a brief overview of the issues associated with assessment and management of depression in the elderly. Treatment interventions include counseling and pharmacology. In addition, the article notes particular attention should be given to side effects of antidepressant medications and possible drug interactions when treating depression in the elderly.

142   Hughes, C.P. (1992). Community psychiatric nursing and depression in elderly people. Journal of Advanced Nursing, 17(1), 34-42.

This article provides an indepth review of the recent literature related to assessment and treatment of depression in older persons. Implications of research findings are then discusses as related to the practice of community psychiatric nursing.

143   Koenig, H.G., & Breitner, J.C. (1990). Use of antidepressants in medically ill older patients. Psychosomatics, 31(1), 22-32.

This article examines the course of major depression in older patients and its effects on the treatment, course, and outcome of physical illness. Counseling is recommended for persons experiencing depression regardless of whether anti-depressants are prescribed as many causes of depression are situational in nature.

144   Priddy, J.M. (1982). Overcoming learned helplessness in elderly clients: Skills training for service providers. Educational Gerontology, 8(5), 507-518.

This article discusses the losses of aging as related to the theory of learned helplessness. Application of these concepts for service providers working with depressed older persons are discussed and the concept of allowing older persons to have an impact within the counseling interaction as a method of reducing helplessness is discussed.

145   Stewart, L. (1986). Letter to the editor. Mental Health in Australia, 1(16), 40.

The author argues for the need to prevent depression in older persons and discusses factors which contribute to depression in this population.

SUBSTANCE ABUSE

146   Brewer, L.G., Zawadski, M.L., & Lincoln, R. (1990). Characteristics of alcoholics and codependents who did and did not complete treatment. International Journal of the Addictions, 25(6), 653-663.

Data collected from 803 patients aged 18-85 revealed that previous counseling and health issues were related to staying in treatment among codependents. Chemical dependents who finished treatment were more likely to be female, employed, and willing to commit themselves to self-help meetings.

147   Doering, B.S. (1991). Another look at older problem drinkers. Journal of Mental Health Counseling, 13(4), 432-434.

This article is a reply to a previous article by Richard Blake entitled "Mental Health Counseling and Older Problem Drinkers." Also includes discussion of abstinence as the overall goal of treatment.

148   Gottheil, E. (1987). Drug use, misuse, and abuse by the elderly. Medical Aspects of Human Sexuality, 21(3), 29-37.

This article describes the epidemiology, assessment, and treatment of drug abuse in older persons. Early intervention and prevention are stressed as the key elements in a treatment program.

149   Hammarlund, E.R., Ostrom, J.R., & Kethley, A.J. (1985). The effects of drug counseling and other educational strategies on drug utilization in the elderly. Medical Care, 23(2), 165-170.

This article reports the results of a study of medication behavior of older persons living in an apartment complex for older persons. It appears that drug counseling is an effective health promotion strategy in this setting.

150   Kelly, S., & Remley, T. (1987). Understanding and counseling elderly alcohol abusers. American Mental Health Counselors Association Journal, 9(2), 105-113.

This study investigated the causes of abusive drinking among older persons. Treatment strategies are reviewed, including abstinence, support groups, and reminiscence therapy.

151   Kofoed, L.L., Tolson, R.L., Atkinson, R.L., & Toth, R.L. (1987). Treatment compliance of older alcoholics: An elder-specific approach is superior to "mainstreaming." Journal of Studies on Alcohol, 48(1), 47-51.

The treatment compliance of 23 male and 2 female alcoholics were studied in an elder-specific treatment program. Significant differences with respect to treatment, retention, compliance, and completion were found for subjects in the elder-specific program.

152   McMahon, R.C., Kouzekanani, K., DeMarco, L.A., & Kusel, S.J. (1992). Cognitive motivations for drinking among alcoholics: Factor structure and correlates. American Journal of Drug and Alcohol Abuse, 18(4), 477-487.

This article explores the reasons for drinking and expectations about the effects of drinking among inpatient alcoholics through the use of the Alcohol Evaluation Instrument. Factors related to negative mood reduction, positive mood enhancement, and social functioning emerged.

SUICIDE

153   Achte, K. (1986). Some psychodynamic aspects of the presuicidal syndrome with special reference to older persons. Crisis, 7(1), 24-32.

This article presents a comprehensive look at psychodynamic aspects of pre-suicidal syndrome and older persons. Suicidal fantasies are compared to self-help medication and the implications of this concept are discussed. In addition, characteristics are identified and discussed of persons with high risk of suicide. Emphasis is placed on application.

154 Coombs, D.W., Miller, H.L., Alarcon, R., Herlihy, C., Lee, J.M., & Morrison, D.P. (1992). **Presuicide attempt communications between parasuicides and consulted caregivers.** Suicide Life Threat Behavior, 22(3), 289-302.

This article discusses presuicide attempt communications and implications.

155 Osgood, N., & McIntosh, J. (1986). Suicide and the Elderly. Westport, CT: Greenwood Press.

This book presents a compilation of references related to the topic of suicide and older persons. An introduction provides an overview of the topic. This is followed by citations and brief annotations arranged by subject.

156 Lester, D. (1993). **Social correlates of suicide and homicide in England: A comparison with the U.S.A.** European Journal of Psychiatry, 7(2), 122-126.

This study examined the social correlates of suicide and homicide in England and the U.S.A. In both countries, suicide rates were lower among people born in-county/in-state. Suicide rates were higher for counties with high concentrations of older persons in England and lower for counties with high concentrations of older persons in the U.S.A. The U.S.A. had a higher suicide rate overall than England.

157 McIntosh, J. (1988-1989). **Official U.S. elderly suicide data bases: Levels, availability, omissions.** Omega Journal of Death and Dying, 19(4), 337-350.

This article presents a thorough review of the available data on level, availability, and omissions related to suicide rates. Older persons are found to be at the highest risk for suicide. Explanations of this finding and limitations of current data bases are included.

158 Mechanic, D., Angel, R., & Davies, L. (1991). **Risk and selection processes between the general and the specialty mental health sectors.** Journal of Health and Social Behavior, 32(1), 49-64.

This article reports the findings of a study investigating risk and selection processes between the general and the specialty mental health sectors. Interestingly, results indicate that risk and a measure of suicide thoughts increase referral to specialty care. Additionally, women and persons with higher education were more likely to use specialty services whereas older persons were less likely to use such services. Implications for practice are discussed.

**159   Watson, W.   (1991).   Ethnicity, crime, & aging: Risk factors and
       adaptation.   Generations, 15(4), 53-57.**

This article presents a review of the literature related to criminal victimization of
and the perpetration of crimes by ethnic older persons.   Results indicated
homicide increases with age after 55 years.   In addition, robbery and purse
snatching were the most likely offenses against older persons.   Suicide and
homicide incident literature is also reviewed.   Implications are discussed.

3

Needs and Services for Older Persons

THE AGING NETWORK SERVICE DELIVERY SYSTEM

160   Cubillos, H.L., Prieto, M.M., & Paz, J.J. (1988). Hispanic elderly and long term care: The community's response. Pride Institute Journal of Long Term Home Health Care, 7(4), 14-21.

This article describes the health needs and health status of the elderly Hispanic population in the U.S. Both social and health care services are needed by this population, including counseling.

161   Lurie, A., & Rich, J.C. (1984). The medical center's impact in the network to sustain the aged in the community. Journal of Gerontological Social Work, 7(3), 65-73.

This article describes efforts by a social work department located in a medical center to define the needs of a high risk elderly population and develop a continuum of comprehensive services to meet these needs. A community-based program model is utilized. Results of this program are discussed.

162   McCoy, H.V., Kipp, C.W., & Ahern, M. (1992). Reducing older patients' reliance on the emergency department. Social Work in Health Care, 17(1), 23-37.

This article discusses the tendency of older persons to utilize hospital emergency departments to avoid mental health services. In addition, an intervention designed to link older persons with appropriate community and hospital resources is presented. Implications for social workers are discussed.

163   Myers, J.E., & Salmon, H. (1984). Counseling programs for older persons: Status, shortcomings, and potentialities. Counseling Psychologist, 12(2), 39-53.

This article describes and discusses a variety of programs and services designed to meet the mental health and psychosocial needs of older adults. Gaps and potentials of the existing service delivery systems are identified.

164   Scharlach, A., Mor-Barak, M., Katz, A., Birba, L., Garcia, G., & Sokolov, J. (1992). Generation: A corporate sponsored retiree health program. Gerontologist, 32(2), 265-269.

This article reports on an innovative program sponsored by Southern California Edison Company for the company's retirees and their dependents. This comprehensive, multidisciplinary program includes both traditional medical care and prevention activities (health education workshops, polypharmacy problems, individual and group counseling, and community resource education).

165   Williams, W.C., & Lair, G.S. (1988). Geroconsultation: A proposed decision-making model. Journal of Counseling and Development, 67(3), 198-201.

This article recognizes the increasing number of older persons in United States Society and the resulting need for consultants trained in the special needs of this population. A consultation model and decision making model are included.

INFORMAL SUPPORT NETWORKS

166   Cain, E., Kohorn, E., Quinlan, D., Latimer, K., & Schwartz, P. (1986). Psychosocial benefits of a cancer support group. CANCER, 57(1), 183-189.

This article describes the psychosocial benefits of a cancer support group. Benefits of group support are emphasized.

167   Koenig, H.G. (1986). Shepherds centers: Helping elderly help themselves. Journal of the American Geriatrics Society, 34(1), 73.

Shepherds centers are community-based support programs for older persons framed through the cooperation of local churches and synagogues. They are described as a cost-effective means of meeting many of the needs of older people, including needs for counseling.

INDEPENDENT LIVING IN COMMUNITY SETTINGS

168 Eisenberg, D.M., & Carilio, T.E. (1990). Friends of the family: Counseling elders at family service agencies. Generations, 14(1), 25-26.

Family service agencies have traditionally been a source of counseling for individuals, couples, and families in coping with the stresses of life, including aging. They can be especially important sources of assistance for older persons living in the community.

169 Grady, S. (1990). Senior centers: An environment for counseling. Generations, 14(1), 15-18.

This article discusses the importance of senior center in providing older persons with services and activities to enhance their quality of life. Gerontological counselors have the opportunity to impact a large number of older persons through contact at these centers.

170 Hereford, R.W. (1989). The market for community services for older persons. Pride Institute Journal of Long Term Home Health Care, 8(1), 44-51.

This article discusses a program of support services for older people that was developed following a survey of services needed by older persons and their caregivers. Counseling was identified as a need in addition to a variety of home-based support services.

171 Kligman, E.W. (1989, November). Multiple risk factor intervention in the delivery of primary health care to the elderly: Lessons from community-based programs. Paper presented at the Annual Meeting of the Gerontological Society, Minneapolis, MN.

This study acknowledges the increasing role of the primary care physician in caregiving to older persons including counseling and education related to health aging. Project AGE WELL, a longitudinal study of a comprehensive health promotion program for older persons, is presented.

172 Lipsman, R., Fader, D., & Harmon, J.S. (1992). Developing home-based mental health services for Maine's older adults. Pride Institute Journal of Long Term Home Health Care, 11(1), 29-38.

This article describes the development of three home-based geriatric mental health programs. Key components of each program include staff recruitment, building community support, and developing linkages with aging network agencies.

173   Rahder, B., Farge, B., & Todres, R. (1992). A review of the Canadian and American literature on homesharing agencies with a service component...unrelated people occupy a single dwelling. Home Health Care Services Quarterly, 13(1/2), 71-90.

This article presents a comprehensive review of the literature related to home sharing agencies. Topics included are types of agencies, activities provided by such agencies, funding, staff, and coordination. Strong links with other community agencies and a clear understanding of the needs of their client population were predictors of success.

ADULT DAY CARE

174   Hedenstrom, J., & Ostwald, S.K. (1988). Adult day care programs: Maintaining a therapeutic triad. Home Health Care Services Quarterly, 9(1), 85-102.

The authors studied 48 adult day care programs in Minnesota, focusing on programs for older persons and patterns of family involvement. Over 75% of the programs operated according to a social/health center model, with counseling being a frequent service provided to participants.

175   Kirwin, P.M. (1985-86). Adult day care: An integrated model. Journal of Gerontological Social Work, 9(2), 59-71.

Integrating adult day care and senior center programs increases participant options while decreasing service cost, and is recommended in planning community service options for frail elderly individuals.

176   Kirwin, P.M., & Kaye, L.W. (1991). Service consumption patterns over time among adult day care program participants. Home Health Care Services Quarterly, 12(4), 45-58.

This study analyzes data from 59 adult day care programs in Pennsylvania. Types of services utilized by clients and the relationship between formal service consumption and the helping behaviors of family caregivers are included.

177   Wallace, S.P., Ingman, S.R., Snyder, J.L., & Planning, M. (1991). The evolving status of adult day care: Evidence for Missouri. Pride Institute Journal of Long Term Home Health Care, 10(4), 30-37.

This article analyzes data from 25 adult day care programs in Missouri. Client and service characteristics are reported. Additionally, programs reported that clients are increasingly more impaired and a need for Medicare funding.

SOCIAL SERVICE NEEDS

178 Burdick, D.C., & Santos, J.F. (1982). Training housing authority personnel: Enhancing social services for aged dwellers. Journal of Applied Gerontology, 1(June), 53-57.

This article discusses the increasing needs of the aging population and the lack of trained personnel to fill these needs. In an alternative strategy to fill this need, the National Institute of Mental Health has begun a program to train housing authority personnel to work with the elderly population. Additionally, program effectiveness is discussed.

179 Burton, L.M. (1992) Black grandparents rearing children of drug-addicted parents: Stressors, outcomes, and social service needs. Gerontologist, 32(6), 744-751.

This article reports the data of two qualitative studies of Black grandparents and great-grandparents who are raising their children's children as a result of drug addiction. The positive and negative impacts of surrogate parenting were discussed.

180 Ekland, S.J., Siffin, C.F., & Stafford, P.B. (1990). Alzheimer's Awareness Days: A community education model. Gerontology and Geriatrics Education, 10(3), 1-10.

This article reports the results of a 1988 community education project based in Indiana. This project serves as a model of university and community cooperation to serve the aging population and suggestions for program implementation in other communities are provided.

181 Eng, E. (1993). The Save our Sisters Project. A social network strategy for reaching rural black women. Cancer, 72(3 Suppl), 1071-1077.

This article describes the results of a study funded by the National Cancer Institute to support a pilot demonstration study in a rural county of North Carolina. This pilot study was designed to increase mammography screening among older Black women and utilized other Black women as "natural helpers" to help reach out to this population. The innovative methods employed in this study are included in the article.

182 Johnson, R.P., & Stripling, R.O. (1984). Bridging the gap between counselor educators and the administrators of programs for the elderly. Counselor Education and Supervision, 23(4), 276-289.

This article reports the results of a survey which targeted gerontological counselor educators and program administrators from Area Agencies on Aging. The results of the study showed a wide gap between the perceptions of counselor educators and program administrators.

183   Kalymun, M. (1990). Toward a definition of assisted-living. Journal of Housing for the Elderly, 7(1), 97-132.

This study reports the findings of a study which explored assisted-living environments in southeastern Florida. Characteristics of the facilities and residents are included. Examples of services provided include meals, personal care, medical assistance, social activities,s security, and transportation.

184   Kent, K.L. (1990). Elders and community mental health centers. Generations, 14(1), 19-21.

The author describes ways in which community mental health centers differ from other settings in which older persons receive mental health care. Client recruitment, reasons older clients seek assistance, and counseling approaches used are discussed.

185   Lustbader, W. (1990). Mental health services in a community health center. Generations, 14(1), 22-23.

This article presents a model for a neighborhood clinic for delivery of joint physical and mental health services to older persons. While initial concerns focus on concrete, physical needs, later sessions evolve into more traditional individual and family psychotherapy sessions.

186   Penn, N.E., Levy, V.L., & Penn, B.P. (1986). Professional services preferred by urban elderly Black women. American Journal of Social Psychiatry, 6(2), 129-130.

The authors assessed perceived needs for professional counseling among 30 elderly Black women. The results substantiate the coping strategies of older Black women developed over the course of a lifetime of adversity.

187   Penning, M., & Wasyliw, D. (1992). Homebound learning opportunities: Reaching out to older shut-ins and their caregivers. Gerontologist, 32(5), 704-707.

This article describes a non-profit health promotion and educational service for homebound older adults, Homebound Learning Opportunities of Manitoba, Canada. An audiovisual lending library, educational television programming, and peer counseling are major program components.

188   Powers, J.S. (1989). Helping family and patients decide between home care and nursing home care. Southern Medical Journal, 82(6), 723-726.

This study discusses the importance of assisting patients and families in making the decision between home care and nursing home care. The importance of the physician's ability to assist patients and their families with this difficult decision is emphasized. Techniques for assisting families and patients with this difficult decision are included.

189   Rosengarten, L. (1986). Creating a health-promoting group for elderly couples on a home health care program. Social Work in Health Care, 11(4), 83-92.

Home health care social workers are in a unique position to develop health promoting groups for frail elderly couples. Such groups can help decrease the chance of nursing home placement.

190   Royse, D., & Dhooper, S.S. (1988). Social services with cancer patients and their families: Implications for independent social workers. Journal of Independent Social Work, 2(3), 63-71.

A survey of social services received by cancer patients of varying ages revealed that younger, divorced, and single/widowed women were most likely to receive services. Supportive counseling was the service most often requested by clients.

191   Van Auken, E. (1991). Crisis intervention: Elders awaiting placement in an acute care facility. Journal of Gerontological Nursing, 17(11), 30-33.

This article discusses crisis intervention techniques for older persons awaiting placement in an acute care facility.

192   Waring, M.L., & Kosberg, J.I. (1984). Morale and the differential use among the black elderly of social welfare services delivered by volunteers. Journal of Gerontological Social Work, 6(4), 81-94.

This article reports on the results of a study of black elders who utilized a Congregate Meals Program in Florida. Results of the study indicate that while the program meets many needs of these individuals, it is not related to morale. Support services such as shopping and transportation were found to be related to high morale.

193   Wright, B., Thyer, B.A., & DiNitto, D. (1985). Health and social welfare needs of the elderly: A preliminary study. Journal of Sociology and Social Welfare, 12(2), 431-439.

A random sample of 75 older adults were surveyed to determine their current and future perceived health and social service needs. Counseling and continuing education were low priorities, while physical health and concrete social services were seen as most needed.

EMPLOYMENT COUNSELING

194   Barclay, T.A., & McDougall, M. (1990).   Older worker programs. Generations, 14(1), 53-54.

This article describes a special project for older workers that included a statewide job hotline, individualized client assessment, skill training, and job search training. Clients are helped to identify transferrable skills and experience improvements in self-esteem through participation in the project.

195   Bornstein, J.M. (1986). Retraining the older worker: Michigan's experience with senior employment services. Journal of Career Development, 13(2), 14-22

This article describes Michigan's attempts to provide employment services to economically disadvantaged persons through federal programs such as the Job Training Partnership Act. A variety of older worker training programs are included.

196   Herbert, J.T., & Dambrocia, C.J. (1989). Employability of persons with disabilities: A partnership among employers, rehabilitation counselors and potential workers. Journal of Applied Rehabilitation Counseling, 20(4), 16-21.

This article examines obstacles to employment experienced by older disabled individuals. The role of rehabilitation counselors is discussed and sources of counselor bias against this client population are considered.

197   Riverin-Simard, D. (1990). Adult vocational trajectory. Career Development Quarterly, 39(2), 129-142.

Interviews with 786 adults aged 23 to 67 provide the basis for a spatial-temporal model of adult vocational development. Phases of occupational life vary between stability and instability.

RETIREMENT COUNSELING

198   Balk, U.J. (1988). Retiring early. Personnel Administration, 33(6), 81-83.

The author argues that early retirees might benefit from outplacement counseling to assist them in dealing with the problems they will face when they retire.

199   Clark, D.J. (1982, March). <u>Retirement satisfaction among coal miners:</u> <u>A correlational study</u>. Paper presented at Annual Meeting of the Southeastern Psychological Association, New Orleans, LA.

The results of a study investigating retirement satisfaction among retired coal minors are presented. Results indicate that when health and adequate income were held constant, planning was the best predictor of retirement satisfaction. This study has implications for retirement and pre-retirement counselors.

200   Fretz, B.R., Kluge, N.A., Ossana, S.M., & Jones, S.M. (1989). Intervention targets for reducing preretirement anxiety and depression. <u>Journal of Counseling Psychology</u>, <u>36</u>(3), 301-307.

The results of a study reported in this article indicate that the best predictors of preretirement worry are a low sense of self-efficacy and a low degree of planfulness, in addition to concerns about money and health. No differences were found between those within 2-3 years of retirement and those currently eligible to retire.

201   Hernan, J.A. (1984). Exploding aging myths through retirement counseling. <u>Journal of Gerontological Nursing</u>, <u>10</u>(4), 31-33.

This article explores the benefits of retirement counseling for the elderly population.

202   Tincher, B.J. (1992). Retirement: perspectives and theory. <u>Physical and Occupational Therapy in Geriatrics</u>, <u>11</u>(1), 55-62.

This article explores the role of occupational therapists in assisting older persons with pre-retirement and retirement counseling. In addition, the article explores issues associated with retirement.

EDUCATION AND AGING

203   Henderson, M. (1990). Beyond the living will. <u>Gerontologist</u>, <u>30</u>(4), 480-485.

This author studied older residents of a retirement community to determine whether planning for and control over the dying process would reduce death anxiety. Those who received counseling and the opportunity to prepare a living will experienced a significant reduction in death anxiety as measured by the Templer Death Anxiety Scale.

204   Housely, W.F. (1992). Psychoeducation for personal control: A key to psychological well-being in the elderly. Educational Gerontology, 18(8), 785-794.

Psychoeducational and other counseling interventions are presented as a means of supporting and maintaining psychological well being in older persons, in spite of the decrements which accompany the aging process. Psychological well-being is related to perceptions of personal control among older adults.

205   Hyde, R.B. (1988). Facilitative communication skills training: Social support for elderly people. Gerontologist, 28(3), 418-420.

Elderly residents of a retirement community were trained in basic helping skills and reported a significant increase in self-perceptions of helpfulness after the training. They also were more able to distinguish between helpful and non-helpful responses.

206   Karl, F. (1991). Outreach counseling and educational activities in a district. Educational Gerontology, 17(5), 487-493.

This article describes a program for outreach counseling in West Germany which encouraged older persons of working class to take part in study groups, lecture courses, and educational excursions. Outreach counseling was effective in encouraging program participation.

207   Kimberlin, C.L., Berardo, D.H., Pendergast, J.F., & McKenzie, L.C. (1993). Med-Care, 31(5), 451-468.

This study discusses the role of the pharmacist in preventing and resolving drug-related problems in patients, particularly in the elderly population. Additionally, the article describes a program designed to teach community pharmacists a process for assessing drug therapy of older clients and a process for intervening to correct problems associated with drug therapy.

208   Links, C., & Frydenberg, H. (1988). Microcomputer skills training program for the physically disabled in long term rehabilitation. Physical and Occupational Therapy in Geriatrics, 6(3-4), 133-140.

A five month microcomputer skills training program in a long term care facility provided a variety of benefits, including increased independent functioning, acquisition of basic computer skills, vocational exploration, and increased self-esteem. While competitive employment may not be a reasonable goal, the training in and of itself might offer therapeutic benefits to rehabilitation patients.

209   Rubin, F.H., & Black, J.S. (1992). Health care and consumer control: Pittsburgh's Town Meeting for seniors. Gerontologist, 32(6), 853-855.

This study reports on semi-annual town meetings conducted by two hospital in Pittsburgh. These meetings are designed to provide community based health education and to increase decision making skills in the elderly population. In addition, these information gathered at these town meetings has resulted in the creation of several new community programs.

LONG TERM CARE IN NURSING HOMES

210   Chatman, V.S., & Turner-Friley, S. (1988). Providing long-term health care to the minority aging poor: A case management approach. Pride International Journal of Long Term Home Health Care, 7(4), 10-12.

Case management is recommended as an effective strategy for providing comprehensive screening, assessment, follow-up, and monitoring services for older Black clients. Counseling is one of many services offered in this model.

211   Clavon, A. (1986). The Black elderly. Journal of Gerontological Nursing, 12(5), 6-12.

Although they represent 11% of the elderly population, Blacks comprise only 3% of the nursing home population. Families of minority elderly need counseling to resolve the issues and value conflicts associated with nursing home placement.

212   Crose, R. (1990). Establishing and maintaining intimate relationships among nursing home residents. Journal of Mental Health Counseling, 12(1), 102-106.

The therapeutic goals for nursing home residents which are discussed in this article include resolution of current conflicts, increase in meaningful social interaction and sense of self-worth, and empowerment. A group therapy intervention model is presented along with case examples demonstrating how the model can be applied to achieve the stated goals.

213   Dierking, B., Brown, M., & Fortune, A.E. (1980). Task-centered treatment in a residential facility for the elderly: A clinical trial. Journal of Gerontological Social Work, 2(3), 225-240.

This article reports on the application of a task-centered, short-term, goal oriented counseling approach in a long-term care facility with an elderly population. The purpose of the approach is to reduce the individual's difficulties in coping with the environment. The article includes case illustrations.

214   Frey, D.E., Kelbley, T.J., Durham, L., & James, J.S. (1992). Enhancing the self-esteem of selected male nursing home residents. Gerontologist, 32(4), 552-557.

This study reports the results of a treatment to increase self-esteem among male nursing home residents. Results indicate that the treatment group had significantly increased self-esteem following treatment however, this came only following a significant decrease in feelings of self-worth due to anxiety.

215   Ganote, S. (1990). A look at counseling in long term care settings. Generations, 14(1), 31-34.

This article provides a discussion of issues related to counseling in long term care settings. Included are subjects such as client profiles, methods of recruitment, interventions, caregiver-client relationships, and a comparison with counseling in other settings.

216   Gottesman, L.E., Peskin, E., Kennedy, K., & Mossey, J. (1991). Implications of a mental health intervention for elderly mentally ill residents of residential care facilities. International Journal of Aging and Human Development, 32(3), 229-245.

This study reports the results of a two year mental health intervention conducted in a residential facility with elderly residents with a history of mental illness. Results of the study are reported and suggestions for future interventions given.

217   Schwanke, E.R. (1986). Providing pastoral care for the elderly in long term care facilities without a chaplain utilizing coordinated congregational resources. Journal of Religion and Aging, 2(3), 57-64.

Twelve church congregations worked together to provide spiritual care in six nursing homes which did not have chaplains. Meaningful visits were made by trained and supervised lay persons as well as trained chaplains.

218   Schwartzben, S.H. (1989). The 10th floor family support group: A descriptive model of the use of a multi-family group in a home for the aged. Social Work With Groups, 12(1), 41-54.

This article describes an effective multifamily group experience in an institutional setting. The families were mutually supportive and were able to effect interventions in the setting on behalf of residents.

219   Spears, R., Drinka, P.J., & Voeks, S.K. (1993). Obtaining a durable power of attorney for health care from nursing home residents. Journal of Family Practice, 36(4), 409-413.

This article reports on a pilot program designed to explore the issues of obtaining a durable power of attorney for health care from nursing home residents. Results of the program and suggestions for future programs are included.

220 Uhlman, J., & Steinke, P.D. (1984). Pastoral visitation to the institutionalized aged: Delivering more than a lick and a promise. Pastoral Psychology, 32(4), 231-238.

This article describes a nationwide study of older persons in nursing homes conducted by the Lutheran Council USA. Older persons did not feel their needs were met in terms of time spent with them by chaplains. Older persons who had few visitors were most vulnerable.

221 Whall, A.L., Gillis, G.L., Yankou, D., Booth, D.E., & Beel-Bates, C.A. (1992). Disruptive behavior in elderly nursing home residents: A survey of nursing staff. Journal of Gerontological Nursing, 18(10), 13-17.

This article explores disruptive behavior in elderly nursing home residents and the perceptions of nursing staff. Staff were asked to list disruptive behaviors as well as their interventions. Results of the study are included.

HOSPICE

222 Etten, M.J., & Kosberg, J.T. (1989). The hospice caregiver assessment: A study of a case management tool for professional assistance. Gerontologist, 29(10, 128-131.

The authors developed the Hospice Caregiver Assessment Inventory to identity the problems of those caring for dying persons. Caregivers to dying older persons most often need counseling both prior to and after the death of their loved one.

223 McCracken, A., & Gerdsen, L. (1991). Sharing the legacy: Hospice care principles for terminally ill elders. Journal of Gerontological Nursing, 17(12), 4-8.

This article describes the Hospice of Cincinnati program for older persons and their families in detail. The objectives are care and physical problems frequently encountered are discussed. Additionally, information on programs for the bereaved family members are included. Emphasis is on application.

4

The Population and Special Situations

OLDER INDIVIDUAL, INTIMACY, AND LONELINESS

Older Women

224   Capuzzi, D., & Friel, S.E. (1990). Current trends in sexuality and aging: An update for counselors. Journal of Mental Health Counseling, 12(2), 342-353.

This article summarizes information concerning the physical and emotional effects of aging on sexuality. Common medical problems that affect the sexuality of older men and women are discussed and implications for counselors are provided.

225   Cavallero, M. (1991). Curriculum guidelines and strategies on counseling older women. Educational Gerontology, 17(2), 157-166.

This author discusses a variety of issues for older women which need to be incorporated into courses in both gerontology and counseling, including health, mental health, family issues, sexuality, widowhood, chemical dependency, and community resources. Both local and national resources are important in counseling older women.

226   Coyle, J. (1989). Women and aging: A selected, annotated bibliography. Westport, CT: Greenwood Press.

This book presents a compilation of references related to the topic of women and aging. An introduction provides an overview of the topic. This is followed by citations and brief annotations arranged by subject.

**227   Crose, R. (1991). What's special about counselling older women?
          Canadian Journal of Counselling, 25(4), 617-623.**

This article discusses the needs of the aging population and gender issues related
to development and late life. In addition, the article discusses the impact of
therapists reliance on personal experience with older persons and the issue of
countertransference.

**228   Cross, R., & Drake, L.K. (1993). Older women's sexuality. Clinical
          Gerontologist, 12(4), 51-56.**

This article combines a discussion of aging and women's sexuality to present a
topic which has become increasingly important in our aging society.

**229   Grady, K.E., Lemkau, J.P., McVay, J.M., & Reisine, S.T. (1992).
          The importance of physician encouragement in breast cancer
          screening of older women. Preventive Medicine, 21(6), 766-780.**

This article reports the results of a study designed to examine the role of the
physician in encouraging older women to participate in breast cancer screening,
specifically mammography and self-examination. Results indicate that physician
encouragement significantly increased the likelihood of older women participating
in such screenings.

**230   Hopper, S.V. (1993). The influence of ethnicity on the health of
          older women. Clinical Geriatric Medicine, 9(1), 231-259.**

This article provides an extensive review of the impact of ethnicity on aging,
specifically, as a buffer and as a filter for the aging experience. Additionally,
counselors are encouraged to seek a deeper understanding of and acknowledge
respect for cultural beliefs and practices when working with older persons from
ethnic groups. Communication strategies for working with older persons from
various ethnic groups are included.

**231   Jamuna, D. (1985). Self-concept among middle-aged and older
          women. Journal of the Indian Academy of Applied Psychology,
          11(2), 16-18.**

A study of the self-concepts of 300 women in 20 villages in India revealed that
postmenopausal women had the lowest self-concepts, pre-menopausal women the
highest, and menopausal women intermediate self-concept scores. Counseling is
recommended before, during, and after the menopausal transition.

**232   Kivett, V.R. (1990). Older rural women: Mythical, forbearing, and
          unsung. Journal of Rural Community Psychology, 11(1), 83-101.**

This author describes the needs, strengths, and contributions of older rural women, using both quantitative and qualitative data. Older rural women are seen as both active and reactive in family, work, and community.

233   Morgan, L.A. (1986). The financial experience of widowed women: Evidence from the LRHS. Gerontologist, 26(6), 663-668.

An examination of reports from 606 Caucasian widows from the Longitudinal Retirement History Survey reveals that many of them were poor and experience with handling money did not decrease their risk of poverty. Less than one-third had received financial counseling as widows.

234   Morrison-Beedy, D., & Robbins, L. (1989). Sexual assessment and the aging female. Nurse Practitioner: American Journal of Primary Health Care, 14(12), 35-39.

This article discusses the impact of aging on female sexuality. Included are issues such as personal and societal values, normal physiological changes, and availability of a partner. Information vital to the assessment of female sexuality in older persons is discussed. Intervention strategies including treatment options and education are presented.

235   Ribeiro, V. (1989). The forgotten generation: Elderly women and loneliness. Recent Advances in Nursing, (25), 20-40.

This article provides an overview of the scientific study of loneliness including a definition of loneliness, taxonomies of loneliness have been proposed, and theoretical approaches defined. Three perspective identified by Peplau and Perlman (1982) are discussed.

236   Schlesinger, R.A. (1990). Midlife transitions among Jewish women: Counseling issues. Special Issue: Jewish women in therapy: Seen but not heard. Women and Therapy, 10(4), 91-100.

This article examined the issue of returning to the workforce through interviews with 22 Jewish women. A model was developed based upon these interviews. The REAL model is defined and explored. Suggestions for counselors are included.

237   Semel, V. (1990). Confrontation with hopelessness: Psychoanalytic treatment of the older woman. Modern Psychoanalysis, 15(2). 215-224.

This article presents the case study of a 63 year old woman in which feelings of hopelessness are resolved through psychoanalytic treatment. The quality of the therapy was changed when the therapist resolved countertransference issues of hopelessness.

238   Tyra, P.A. (1993). Older women: victims of rape. Journal of Gerontologic Nursing, 19(5), 7-12.

The issues surrounding older women who are victims of rape are explored from a nursing perspective. Rape trauma syndrome, a nursing diagnosis, is defined and explored. Implications and intervention strategies for nurses are included such as identifying victims during routine exams, referring victims for ongoing counseling, etc.

Sexuality and Aging

239   Brandt, K.D., & Potts, M.K. (1987). Arthritis in the elderly: Assessment and management of sexual problems. Medical Aspects of Human Sexuality, 21(3), 57-67.

This article describes the assessment and treatment of sexual problems in older persons with arthritis. Case studies are presented which emphasize the need to encourage older arthritic clients to view sexual involvement in terms of giving and receiving pleasure rather than genital intercourse.

240   Brown, L. (1989). Is there sexual freedom for our aging population in long term care institutions? Journal of Gerontological Social Work, 13(3-4), 75-93.

Older persons have sexual needs which are not being met by long-term care institutions. Counseling concerning intimacy is needed as well as staff training in sexuality issues.

241   Burgener, S., & Logan, G. (1989). Sexuality concerns of the post-stroke patient. Rehabilitation Nursing, 14(4), 178-181.

This article reviews the research related to sexuality in the post-stroke patient and research findings are related to important issues for healthcare providers to consider in rehabilitation of post-stroke patients.

242   Capuzzi, D., & Friel, S.E. (1990). Current trends in sexuality and aging: An update for counselors. Journal of Mental Health Counseling, 12(2), 342-353.

This article summarizes information concerning the physical and emotional effects of aging on sexuality. Common medical problems that affect the sexuality of older men and women are discussed and implications for counselors are provided.

243   Capuzzi, D., & Gossman, L. (1982). Sexuality and the elderly: A group counseling model. Journal for Specialists in Group Work, 7(4), 251-259.

This article provides a description of a group counseling model designed to facilitate the exploration of the issues of sexuality for older adults. The article includes information pertaining to issues such as member selection, leadership style, and length and setting of the group.

244   Catania, J.A. (1989). Issues in AIDS primary prevention for late-middle-aged and elderly Americans. Generations, 13(4), 50-54.

This article presents a three-step, prevention model aimed at risk reduction of Acquired Immune Deficiency Syndrome in older adults. The three steps consist of mass media information, group counseling and education, and teaching communication skills.

245   Cox, J.A. (1986). "Aunt Grace can't have babies." Journal of Religion and Health, 25(1), 73-85.

The author interviewed his elderly aunt concerning her feelings about a miscarriage, stillbirth, newborn death, and false pregnancy 50 years earlier. Her comments lend credibility to coping strategies now being taught to younger persons.

246   Cross, R., & Drake, L.K. (1993). Older women's sexuality. Clinical Gerontologist, 12(4), 51-56.

This article combines a discussion of aging and women's sexuality to present a topic which has become increasingly important in our aging society.

247   Goldstein, H., & Runyon, C. (1993). An occupational therapy educational module to increase sensitivity about geriatric sexuality. Physical and Occupational Therapy in Geriatrics, 11(2), 57-76.

This article presents an overview of a model designed to increase sensitivity regarding geriatric sexuality in students enrolled in occupational therapy programs. The model consists of both didactic and experiential components and has four purposes. This include familiarizing students with normal changes associated with aging and sexuality, dispelling common myths regarding sexuality and aging, understanding the occupational therapists' role in sexual counseling and education, and providing treatment suggestions.

248   Hammond, D.B., & Bonney, W.C. (1985). Results of sex education for support persons working with the elderly. Journal of Sex Education and Therapy, 11(2), 42-45.

Twenty-eight participants in a course on sexuality and aging developed more liberal attitudes while a control group showed no changes. Group participants felt more able to deal openly with older persons relative to sexuality issues.

249   Jain, H., Shamoian, C.A., & Mobarak, A. (1987). Sexual disorders of the elderly. Medical Aspects of Human Sexuality, 21(3), 14-25.

Assessment and treatment of sexual disorders in older persons are discussed, with normal and abnormal sexual responses described. The effects of physical illness, disability, and medications on sexual functioning are considered.

250   Kellett, J.M. (1991). Sexuality of the elderly. Sexual and Marital Therapy, 6(2), 147-155.

The conclusion from a review of research on sexual behavior in older persons is that reduced sexual activity is more cultural than biological in origin. Treatment involves education about normal changes of aging and discussion concerning sexual taboos.

251   Mulligan, T., & Palguta, R.F. (1991). Sexual interest, activity, and satisfaction among male nursing home residents. Archives of Sexual Behavior, 20(2), 199-204.

This article discusses the results of a study investigating sexual interest, activity, and satisfaction among male nursing home residents (n=61) through the use of interviews. Results indicated two-thirds of the subjects expressed an interest in sexual activity, although interest was higher among subjects with a partner, and a preference for coitus as opposed to other methods of sexual expression. Positive correlates of sexual satisfaction included frequency, functional status, and age.

252   Plaut, S.M., Hetherington, S.E., & Ephross, P.H. (1986). Abstracts of sexuality articles by medical, nursing, and social work students: Preferences for journal and topic. Journal of Sex Research, 22(4), 525-531.

Students of medicine, nursing, and social work were asked to submit abstracts on articles of their choice over a two year period. The most frequent topics of study among the students were physical illness and disability, counseling and therapy, and aging, according to an analysis of 760 abstracts from independent annotated bibliographies.

253   Relf, M.V. (1991). Sexuality and the older bypass patient. <u>Geriatric Nursing: American Journal of Care for the Aging</u>, <u>12</u>(6), 294-296.

This article discusses nursing implications associated with issues surrounding sexuality and the older bypass patient.

254   Rienzo, B.A. (1985). The impact of aging on human sexuality. <u>Journal of School Health</u>, <u>55</u>(2), 66-68.

This article discusses the impact of aging on human sexuality and the importance of education for lay persons and professionals regarding these issues. Effective communication techniques and accurate information are presented as key components which can lead to the prevention of psychosocial problems and sexual dysfunction.

255   Schover, L.R. (1993). Sexual rehabilitation after treatment for prostate cancer. <u>Cancer</u>, 71(3 Suppl), 1024-1030.

This article indicates the need for counseling of the patient and sexual partners as part of the rehabilitation process in patients receiving treatments for prostate cancer.

256   Smedly, G. (1991). Addressing sexuality in the elderly. <u>Rehabilitation Nursing</u>, <u>16</u>(1), 9-11.

This article discusses the need for rehabilitation nurses to be sensitive to the issues of sexuality when working with older persons. Sexual assessment and counseling are presented as important components in the rehabilitation process.

257   Spica, M.M. (1992). Educating the client on the effects of COPD on sexuality: The role of the nurse. <u>Sexuality and Disability</u>, <u>10</u>(2), 91-101.

This article presents a model for nurses to educate clients on the effects of COPD on sexuality. In addition, data from a study employing this model are presented. Education and sexuality counseling are important components of this model.

258   Talashek, M.L., Tichy, A.M., & Epping, H. (1990). Sexually transmitted diseases in the elderly: Issues and recommendations. <u>Journal of Gerontological Nursing</u>, <u>16</u>(4), 33-40.

Preventive health care is recommended as the primary strategy required to reduce the prevalence of sexually transmitted diseases in the older population. Counseling is an essential element in primary, secondary, and tertiary prevention strategies.

259   Waterhouse, J., & Metcalfe, M. (1991). Attitudes toward nurses discussing sexual concerns with patients. Journal of Advanced Nursing, 16(9), 1048-1054.

This article discusses the results of a research study conducted to assess patient attitudes toward nurses discussing sexual concerns with patients. Results indicated that 92% of the subjects thought that nurses should discuss sexual concerns with clients. Number of other with whom sexual concerns are discussed and race were found to be significant predictors of attitudes.

260   Whitnourne, S. (1990). Sexuality in the aging male. Generations, 14(3), 28-30.

This article presents an overview of the physiological and psychological changes associated with male sexuality and aging. Normal changes associated with aging as well as certain pathology which may affect sexuality are discussed. Implications for couples are also included.

261   Wise, T., Epstein, S., & Ross, R. (1992). Sexual issues in the medically ill and aging. Psychiatric Medicine, 10(2), 169-80.

This article discusses the issues of sexuality in a population of medically ill and aging individuals.

Intimate Relationships and Single Living

262   Beckham, K., & Giordano, J.A. (1986). Illness and impairment in elderly couples: Implications for marital therapy. Family Relations Journal of Applied Family and Child Studies, 35(2), 257-264.

The impact of disabling illnesses and impairments on marital relationships in later life are examined. Barriers to treatment in both older clients and their therapists are considered and suggestions for overcoming these barriers are provided.

263   Gafner, G. (1987). Engaging the elderly couple in marital therapy. American Journal of Family Therapy, 15(4), 305-315.

The dramatic increases in numbers of older persons will result in increased needs for marriage and family therapists to be skilled in working with this population. Assessment and treatment issues are discussed, along with a case presentation.

264   Gafner, G. (1987). Paradoxical marital therapy and the discouragement meter. Clinical Gerontologist, 6(3), 67-70.

This article describes the marital therapy of a 66 year old man with intractable depression and his wife of 39 years. The couple were presented with a discouragement meter to help guage changes in their problems.

265 **Greenbaum, J., & Rader, L. (1989). Marital problems of the "old" elderly as they present to a mental health clinic. Journal of Gerontological Social Work, 14(1-2), 111-126.**

This article explores the mental health problems faced by older couples and interventions which may best meet their needs. Case examples demonstrate the difficulties in getting couples to communicate and agree upon their problems and solutions.

Loss and Grief

266 **Crane, F.W., & Kramer, B.J. (1987). Perceptions of losses in the later years. Counseling and Values, 31(2), 185-159.**

The perceptions of 447 service providers and 983 older adults relative to the seriousness of 21 losses were compared. Responses of the two groups differed significantly, suggesting that older adults become more proactive in their treatment programs and service providers re-examine the content of their pre- and in-service training programs.

267 **Horacek, B. (1991). Toward a more viable model of grieving and consequences for older persons. Death Studies, 15(5), 459-472.**

This article reviews theories of grief and suggests that the traditional models of grief inadequately explain the process in a simplistic manner. An alternative model is proposed and it is further argued that when high grief deaths occur, the bereaved may eventually be able to adjust to the loss however, the grieving process may persist indefinitely. Implications of the proposed model for older persons are discussed.

268 **Kalish, R. (1987). Older people and grief. Special issue: Death and bereavement. Generations, 11(3), 33-38.**

This article discusses the experiences of loss and grief among older persons. Several aspects of the grief/loss experience are discussed including cognitive, affective, physical, and behavioral expressions.

269 **Jacobs, S., Mason, J., Kosten, T., & Wahby, V. (1986). Bereavement and catecholamines. Journal of Psychosomatic Research, 30(4), 489-496.**

The results of a study investigating the relationship between catecholamines and bereavement are reported. The expected relationship between psychological distress and catecholamine output was not found. Implications are discussed.

**270   Valanis, B., Yeaworkth, R., & Mullis, M.   (1987).   Alcohol use
          among bereaved and nonbereaved older persons.   Journal of
          Gerontological Nursing, 13(5), 26-32.**

This article reports the findings of a study which examined alcohol use among
bereaved and nonbereaved older persons. Results indicated prevalence of alcohol
use was higher among bereaved older persons.

271   Waltman, R. (1992). When a spouse dies. Nursing, 22(7), 48-51.

This article discusses nursing implications and interventions related to death of
a spouse.

**272   Zisook, S., Shuchter, S., Sledge, P., & Mulvihill, M.   (1993).   Aging
          and bereavement.   Journal of Geriatric Psychiatry and Neurology,
          6(3), 137-143.**

This article reports the findings of a study of grief responses in 350 widows and
widowers.   The effects of age on depressive and anxiety symptoms and
syndromes was studied.   Results indicated that older widows and widowers
reported better adjustment and few anxiety and depressive symptoms than
younger widows and widowers.

Widowhood and Survivorship

**273   Solie, L.J., & Fielder, L.J. (1987-88). The relationship between sex
          role identity and a widow's adjustment to the loss of a spouse.
          Omega Journal of Death and Dying, 18(1), 33-40.**

The results of this study suggest a relationship between behavioral flexibility as
reflected in sex-role identity and loss adjustment. Undifferentiated women,
identified using the BEM Sex Role Inventory, were significantly more well
adjusted and less depressed that were undifferentiated, feminine, or masculine
women.

Divorce

**274   Crose, R., & Duffy, M. (1988). Separation as a therapeutic strategy
          in marital therapy with older couples. Clinical Gerontologist, 8(1),
          71-73.**

This article describes a case study in which marital separation was effected after
50 years of conflict. The health of both partners was threatened prior to the
separation.

275   **Gafner, G. (1989). Marital therapy with an old-old couple. Clinical Gerontologist, 8(4), 51-53.**

This article describes the case of an older couple, married 66 years, who sought martial therapy. Progress was short-lived and separation was suggested.

276   **Shamoian, C.A., & Thurston, F.D. (1986). Marital discord and divorce among the elderly. Medical Aspects of Human Sexuality, 20(8), 25-34.**

Primary care physicians are most likely to be consulted about marital discord among older couples and should be prepared to refer patients for counseling. While the divorce rate in later life is low, the effects on divorcing couples may be devastating.

FAMILY RELATIONSHIPS IN LATER LIFE

277   **Banks, J., Cameron, W., Montague, M., Toliver, J., Hobbs, S., Peterson, L., & Williams, R. (1989). The chronically ill grandparent in minority multigenerational family households: problems and solutions from three points of view. Journal of the National Black Nurses' Association, 3(2), 41-48.**

This article presents the results of a descriptive correlational study of minority multigenerational family household with a chronically ill grandparent using the Interactional Model of Family Systems. Interviews were conducted with the elder family member, adult child, and grandchild. Results include ambivalent feelings, dissatisfaction with relationships with other family members, not feeling needed, and feelings of loneliness. Implications for the design of counseling interventions are included.

278   **Halm, M.A. (1992). Support and reassurance needs: Strategies for practice. Critical Care Nursing Clinics of North America, 4(4), 633-643.**

This article discusses the importance of the healthcare practitioner (critical care nurse) in providing social support to family members of a critically ill patient through family assessment, counseling, and support groups.

279   **Gonzalez, S., Steinglass, P., & Reiss, D. (1989). Putting the illness in its place: Discussion groups for families with chronic medical illnesses. Family Process, 28(1), 63-87.**

The authors describe a new psychosocial intervention for families and patients experiencing the chronic phases of disabling illnesses. A short-term, highly structured, psychoeducationally oriented, multiple family discussion group was successful with a wide range of disabling conditions.

280   McCarthy, B., Kuipers, L., Hurry, J., & Harper, R. (1989). Counseling the relatives of the long-term mentally ill: A low cost supportive model. British Journal of Psychiatry, 154, 775-782.

This article describes a counseling and support group which was implemented for relatives of older persons seen in adult day care programs. The intervention was effective in helping to alleviate emotional reactions to caregiving.

281   Sterns, H.L., Weis, D.M., & Perkins, S.E. (1984). A conceptual approach to counseling older adults and their families. Counseling Psychologist, 12(2), 55-61.

Organized planning and action are required to assist families in dealing with the aging process and its effects on individual family members. The effectiveness of family functioning must be assessed prior to developing a treatment plan.

282   Tresch, D.D., Sims, F.H., & Edmund, H. (1991). Patients in a persistent vegetative state: Attitudes and reactions of family members. Journal of the American Geriatrics Society, 39(1), 17-21.

This study examined the attitudes and reactions of family members to patients in persistent vegetative states. Most family members were committed to the survival of the patient and indicated desires for counseling.

Adult Children and Aging Parents

283   Anastas, J.W., Gibeau, J.L., & Larson, P.L. (1990). Working families and eldercare: A national perspective in an aging America. Social Work, 35(5), 405-411.

This article presents the results of an extensive study investigating the impact of eldercare on working families. Results of the study indicate the women spend more time in caregiving activities and report higher levels of family-work conflict than do men. Recommendations for interventions by social workers are discussed including information and education, counseling, and advocacy.

284   Flori, D.E. (1989). The prevalence of later life family concerns in the marriage and family therapy literature (1976-1985: A content analysis. Journal of Marital and Family Therapy, 15(3), 289-297.

This study reports the results of an examination of Family Process and Journal of Marital and Family Therapy journals from 1976-1985. The purpose of the review was to examine the frequency of coverage on issues related to problems of aging in the family context. Results indicated a lack of coverage of these issues and the authors conclude this is a new frontier for family therapy.

285   Green, C.P. (1991). Clinical considerations: Midlife daughters and their aging parents. Journal of Gerontological Nursing, 17(11), 6-12.

The author discusses the context within which mid-life women address parent-care issues. Group interventions may be especially helpful for these women in addressing their multiple counseling needs.

286   Helfrich, T.E., & Dodson, J.L. (1992). Eldercare: An issue for corporate America. Journal of Case Management, 1(1), 26-29.

This study reports the results of an analysis of secondary data to explore the impact of eldercare on employees. Results indicate a growing number of employees are engaged in caregiving, these activities contribute to employee absenteeism, tardiness, increased use of health benefits, and decreased productivity. Programs developed by corporate America to address these issues are discussed.

287   Myers, J.E. (1988). The mid/late life generation gap" Adult children and aging parents. Journal of Counseling and Development, 66(7), 331-335.

This article suggests that conflicts between adult children and their aging parents are the result of a combination of personal and psychosocial needs, and are amenable to counseling interventions. Strategies for intervention are considered, and the need for counselors to balance the concerns of adult children and aging parents is discussed.

288   Myers, J.E. (1989). Adult children and aging parents. Alexandria, VA: American Counseling Association.

This book was written for counselors and others working with adult children caring for aging parents. Topics included are normative developmental issues in later life, issues related to aging (depression, suicide, substance abuse), psychosocial concerns of caregivers and adult children, family stress situations, and several counseling interventions.

289   Scharlach, A.E. (1987, March). Relieving feelings of burden among women with elderly mothers. Paper presented at the Annual Meeting of the American Society on Aging, Salt Lake City, Utah.

This paper discusses the results of a study designed to test the hypothesis that feelings of burden experienced by adult daughters may interfere with the nature of the daughter's relationship with her aging mother and may result in deleterious effects on the mother. A pre-test, post-test research design was utilized to evaluate two treatment groups and a waiting list control group. Results indicated the cognitive-behavioral intervention was more effective than the supportive-educational intervention or the control group in reducing the daughter's burden, improving the mother-daughter relationship, and decreasing the mother's loneliness.

290   Schmidt, M.G. (1980). Failing parents, aging children. Journal of Gerontological Social Work, 2(3), 259-268.

This article examines issues related to family caregiving for aging family members. Counseling strategies and brief case illustrations are included.

291   Smith, G.C., & Tobin, S.S. (1989, November). How case managers perceive older parents as caregivers of developmentally disabled adult offsprings. Paper presented at the Annual Scientific Meeting of the Gerontological Society, Minneapolis, MN.

This article presents the results of pilot study including ll intensive interviews with case managers about their work with parents of developmentally disabled adults. Results indicate several issues related to aging parents as caregivers of their developmentally disabled adult children. Additionally, results indicate the need for geriatric specialists to serve both aging developmentally disabled clients and their elderly caregivers.

Caregivers to Older Persons

292   Caserta, M.S., Connelly, J.R., Lund, D.A., & Poulton, J.L. (1987). Older adult caregivers of developmentally disabled household members: Service needs and fulfillment. Journal of Gerontological Social Work, 10(1-2), 35-50.

This article reports the results of a study which examined the service needs and level of fulfillment for older adult caregivers of developmentally disabled household members. Information was obtained using indepth, in-home interviews. Results indicated a significant need for key services including housekeeping, home repairs, personal counseling, legal services, and medical doctor services. Implications for future interventions and policy are included.

293   Cox, C., & Ephross, P.H. (1989). Group work with families of nursing home residents: Its socialization and therapeutic functions. Journal of Gerontological Social Work, 13(3-4), 61-73.

Group interventions with families of nursing home residents permit family members to express and deal with negative emotions that often accompany placement of an older relative. Guilt and stress are reduced, and new roles and behaviors appropriate to the institution may be learned.

294   Dellasega, C. (1991). Caregiving stress among community caregivers for the elderly: Does institutionalization make a difference? Journal of Community Health Nursing, 8(4), 197-205.

This article reports the results of a study of caregivers for the elderly, 31 who had place their older person in a nursing home and 93 who had not. Results indicated no significant differences in total score, role or personal strain as measured by the Burden Interview. Implications for nurses and healthcare professionals are discussed.

295   Eisdorfer, C., Rabines, P., & Reisberg, B. (1991). Alzheimer's disease: Caring for the caregiver. Patient Care, 25(18), 109-116, 121-123.

This article discusses an important aspect of working with Alzheimer's disease which may be overlooked, caring for the caregiver. Interventions are discussed.

296   Hamlet, E., & Read, S. (1990). Caregiver education and support group: A hospital based group experience. Journal of Gerontological Social Work, 15(1-2), 75-88.

A support group for caregivers to older persons is described. Key elements of the group included providing emotional support, developing social networks, educating caregivers about normal aging, and problem solving.

297   Marples, M. (1986). Helping family members cope with a senile relative. Social Casework, 67(8), 490-498.

Family members need assistance in coping with the senility of a relative. Individual therapy, educational, and support group interventions are presented as possible means of assistance.

298   Piktialis, D.S. (1990). Employers and elder care: A model corporate program. Pride Institute Journal of Long Term Home Health Care, 9(1), 26-31.

This article describes a model corporate program designed to help both employees and retirees cope with elder care responsibilities. The model is based on consultation, counseling, referral, and identification of resources.

299   Scharlach, A.E. (1989). A comparison of employed caregivers of cognitively impaired and physically impaired elderly persons. Research on Aging, 11(2), 225-243.

This study compared employed caregivers for older persons with Alzheimer's disease with employed caregivers for physically impaired persons. Caregivers for cognitively impaired older persons were more likely to report high levels of emotional, physical, and financial strain.

300   Segall, M., & Wykle, M. (1988-89). The Black family's experience with dementia. Journal of Applied Social Sciences, 13(1), 170-191.

Fifty-eight Black family caregivers for relatives with dementia were interviewed to determine problems, stresses, and coping strategies. Religious faith was a primary means of support, and needs for information, counseling, and respite services were identified.

301   Smith, G.C., Smith, M.F., & Toseland, R.W. (1991). Problems identified by family caregivers in counseling. Gerontologist, 31(1), 15-22.

This study reports the results of a content analysis of counseling problems presented by caregiving daughters and daughters-in-law. Results indicated seven categories including improving coping skills, meeting elder's care needs, responding to family issues, concern over the caregiver-elder relationship, eliciting formal and informal supports, feelings of inadequacy and guild, and planning for elder's future. In addition, case scenarios and implications for counseling are presented.

302   Smith, M.F., Tobin, S.S., & Toseland, R.W. (1992). Therapeutic processes in professional and peer counseling of family caregivers of frail elderly people. Social Work, 37(4), 345-351.

A study comparing the therapeutic processes utilized by peer counselors and professional counselors when counseling caretakers of the elderly is discussed. The study found that professional counselors tended to be friendlier and more willing to give advice than peer counselors.

303   Sutcliffe, C., & Larner, S. (1988). Counselling caregivers of the elderly at home: A preliminary study. British Journal of Clinical Psychology, 27(2), 177-178.

This article reports the results of a study comparing in-home counseling approaches for caregivers of older persons with dementia. Those receiving emotional support experienced a greater reduction in stress than those receiving information only.

304   Wykle, M., & Segal, M. (1991). A comparison of Black and White family caregivers experience with dementia. Journal of Black Nurses' Association, 5(1), 29-41.

This article reports the results of a descriptive study designed to examine Black and White family caregivers experiences related to caring for a relative with dementia. Results indicate differences between the Black and White caregivers in identifying the single-most difficult problem associated with caregiving and differences in coping strategies. Black caregivers tended to rely on religious supports whereas White caregivers tended to seek help from professionals and problem-solving methods. Implications for interventions are discussed.

Elder Abuse

305   **Kallman, H. (1987). Detecting abuse in the elderly. <u>Medical Aspects of Human Sexuality</u>, <u>21</u>(3), 89-99.**

The author presents a series of clues for identifying abuse/neglect and sexual abuse/rape in older persons. The importance of accurate assessment, family interventions, and focusing on the desires of the older client are important in treatment.

306   **Kinderknecht, C.N. (1986). In home social work with abused or neglected elderly: An experiential guide to assessment and treatment. <u>Journal of Gerontological Social Work</u>, <u>9</u>(3), 29-42.**

The author presents practical strategies for assessing and treating abused or neglected older person receiving home health care services. Counseling is described as an important intervention for older persons living with their families.

307   **Myers, J.E., & Shelton, B. (1987). Abuse and older persons: Issues and implications for counselors. <u>Journal of Counseling and Development</u>, <u>65</u>(7), 376-380.**

Characteristics of older persons and their abusers are described and implications for counselors are explored. Counselors need to be prepared to provide both accurate information and resources for all family members in abusive situations.

308   **Powell, S., & Berg, R.C. (1987), When the elderly are abused: Characteristics and intervention. <u>Educational Gerontology</u>, <u>13</u>(1), 71-83.**

The authors examined elder abuse through a systematic review of 60 cases. Multiple types of abuse occurred in most cases. Legal services were the most commonly refused type of assistance.

309   **Schlesinger, J.L., & Salamon, M.J. (1988). A case of wife abuse in the intermediate care facility. <u>Clinical Gerontologist</u>, <u>7</u>(3-4), 163-166.**

This article describes the case of an elderly couple who decided to marry while independent residents of an intermediate care facility. Both refused to be separated but agreed to marital therapy when spouse abuse by the husband became evident.

310   Sengstock, M.C., & Barett, S. (1986). Elderly victims of family
        abuse, neglect, and maltreatment: Can legal assistance help?
        Journal of Gerontological Social Work, 9(3), 43-61.

A study of victims of elder abuse revealed that most were victims of multiple
forms of abuse. Counseling is critical, as is legal intervention for abused older
persons.

LIFESTYLE ISSUES FOR OLDER PERSONS

311   Sennott-Miller, L., & Kligman, E.W. (1992). Healthier lifestyles:
        How to motivate older patients to change. Geriatrics, 47(12), 52-59.

This article discusses the role of the office-based physician in motivating older
patients to change unhealthy lifestyles. A model which includes patient
assessment, discussion of risk and delivery of a message to change, a prescription
for change, and prevention of relapse through a maintenance program is
presented.

Leisure Counseling

312   Balk, U.J. (1988). Retiring early. Personnel Administration, 33(6),
        81-83.

The author argues that early retirees might benefit from outplacement counseling
to assist them in dealing with the problems they will face when they retire.

313   Fretz, B.R., Kluge, N.A., Ossana, S.M., & Jones, S.M. (1989).
        Intervention targets for reducing preretirement anxiety and
        depression. Journal of Counseling Psychology, 36(3), 301-307.

The results of a study reported in this article indicate that the best predictors of
preretirement worry are a low sense of self-efficacy and a low degree of
planfulness, in addition to concerns about money and health. No differences were
found between those within 2-3 years of retirement and those currently eligible
to retire.

314   Leitner, M.J., & Leitner, S.F. (1985). Leisure in later life: A
        sourcebook for provision of recreation services for the elderly.
        Activities, Adaptation, and Aging, 7(3-4), 341.

The various means and settings in which recreation services for older persons
may be provided are reviewed. Leisure counseling is seen as a viable component
of leisure services programs.

Career Counseling for Older Workers

315   Burr, E.W. (1986). What next after fifty? Journal of Career
        Development, 13(2), 23-29.

Techniques appropriate to helping older adults achieve a better lifestyle are
described. These include accepting the past, identifying strengths and limitations,
evaluating and prioritizing choices, and developing plans of action.

316   Cahill, M., & Salamone, P. (1987). Career counseling for work life
        extension: Integrating the older worker in the labor force. Career
        Development Quarterly., 35(3), 188-196.

This article discusses issues involved in older worker retirement and/or
reintegration into the labor market. A variety of options for older workers are
presented and implications for career counseling are considered.

317   Hanson, R.O., Briggs, S.R., & Rule, B.L. (1990). Old age and
        unemployment: Predictors of perceived control, depression, and
        loneliness. Journal of Applied Gerontology, 9(2), 230-240.

This study explored predictors of perceived control, depression, and loneliness
among chronically unemployed older adults. Unemployment counseling is
recommended to help differentiate situational from personality variables related
to adjustment reactions.

318   Holland, J.L. (1982, August). Some implications of career theory for
        adult development and aging. Paper presented at the Annual
        Convention of the American Psychological Association, Washington,
        DC.

This paper presents structural-interactive vocational theory as a model for
conceptualizing career stability and change over the lifespan. Implications for
mental health and vocational service providers are discussed.

319   Kieffer, J.B. (1986). Kicking the premature retirement habit.
        Journal of Career Development, 13(2), 39-51.

This article discusses the origins and consequences of early retirement. An
extended work life is recommended in the future for potential retirees, especially
those for whom the health and economic benefits of work are important.

320   Kouri, M.K. (1986). A life design process for older adults. Journal
        of Career Development, 13(2), 6-13.

A life design process that helps older persons seeking reengagement at various
life stages is described. The process, which includes a 12 hour course or one-to-

one counseling, is effective in helping older people direct their lives in purposeful and meaningful ways.

321   Olson, S.K., & Donovan-Rogers, J. (1986). Resources for career counselors of older adults. _Journal of Career Development_, _13_(2), 57-62.

A 15-item annotated bibliography of information for use in career counseling of older adults is presented. Journals, books, workbooks and informational packets published from 1981-1986 are included.

322   Olson, S.K., & Robbins, S.B. (1986). Guidelines for the development and evaluation of career services for the older adult. _Journal of Career Development_, _13_(2), 63-73.

The authors provide three guidelines for the development and evaluation of career services for older adults. These include using theory as a guide, establishing a hierarchy of objectives, and considering possible attribute and intervention interactions.

323   Sommerstein, J.C. (1986). Assessing the older worker: _Journal of Career Development_, _13_(2), 52-56.

The author describes a variety of instruments and methods which can be adapted for use in career counseling with older adults. These include several published interest inventories and career assessment scales.

Aging in Rural Areas

324   Scheidt, R.J., & Norris-Baker, C. (1990). A transactional approach to environmental stress among older residents of rural communities: Introduction to a special issue. _Journal of Rural Community Psychology_, _11_(1), 5-30.

This article discusses a transactional approach to environmental stress, identifying and taxonomizing multilevel positive and negative outcomes experienced by elderly rural town residents. Implications for professionals working with rural elderly are included.

Responses to Crime

325   Burke, M.J., & Hayes, R.L. (1986). Peer counseling for elderly victims of crime and violence. _Journal for Specialists in Group Work_, _11_(2), 107-113.

Two programs in Illinois are described which are designed to train older persons as volunteers to counsel other older persons in methods of self-protection. Participants report increases in communication skills, knowledge of community services, and problem solving abilities.

326   Cash, T., & Valentine, D. (1987). A decade of adult protective services: Case characteristics. Journal of Gerontological Social Work, 10(3-4), 47-60.

This article reviews 17,355 adult protective services case reports in South Carolina between 1974 and 1984. Counseling and mental health services are recommended to assist victims of maltreatment, neglect, abuse, and exploitation.

5

Theories and Technologies for Counseling Older Persons

327 Agresti, A. (1990). Cognitive screening of the older client. Journal of Mental Health Counseling, 12(3), 384-392.

This article outlines the purposes and goals of cognitive screening with older clients. Common misconceptions regarding late-life cognitive functioning and the necessity for thorough assessment are emphasized.

328 Aranda, M.P. (1990). Culture-friendly services for Latino elders. Generations, 14(1), 55-57.

This article describes a bilingual and bicultural mental health program designed to meet the mental health needs of Spanish speaking older persons in Los Angeles. Counseling is among the array of culture-friendly services provided.

329 Atchley, R.C. (1992). What do social theories of aging offer counselors? Counseling Psychologist, 20(2), 336-340.

This article provides a commentary on Fry's review of social aging theories, suggesting that Fry attempted to cover too many theories, some marginally useful or even discredited, while social breakdown theory was not included.

330 Babins, L. (1988). Conceptual analysis of validation therapy. International Journal of Aging and Human Development, 26(3), 161-168.

Validation therapy is presented as a humanistic approach used to give disoriented, very old people an opportunity to resolve unfinished conflicts through expression of their feelings. The relationship between the older person and the therapist is emphasized, with empathy, acceptance, and acknowledgement among the key interventions used.

331 Babins, L.H., Dillion, J.P., & Merovitz, S. (1988). The effects of validation therapy on disoriented elderly. Activities, Adaptation, and Aging, 12(1-2), 73-86.

The effects of validation therapy were studied using 12 disoriented institutionalized older women aged 80-91. Resulted showed no cognitive changes but some social improvements over the last three of 22 sessions.

332 Barstow, C. (1986). Tending body and spirit: Counseling with elders. Hakomi-Forum, 4, 42-51.

The author addresses older persons, their caregivers, and massage therapists with little background in basic counseling skills. Suggestions for communication strategies to enhance their ability to talk with older people are included.

333 Brown, M.T. (1989). A cross-sectional analysis of self-disclosure patterns. Journal of Mental Health Counseling, 11(4), 384-395.

Developmental counseling approaches are recommended based on the results of this study, which suggest that aging has a positive affect on self-disclosure patterns. Older persons more readily self-disclose in counseling sessions than do younger persons.

334 Burgio, L., & Gurgio, K. (1986). Behavioral gerontology: Application of behavioral methods to the problems of older adults. Journal of Applied Behavioral Analysis, 19(4), 321-328.

This article reviews the current state of areas within behavioral gerontology which require further research. Implications for application are discussed and modifications of therapy which may be necessitated by physiological changes of aging are included.

335 Bowman, G. (1992). Using therapeutic metaphor in adjustment counseling. Journal of Visual Impairment and Blindness, 86(10), 440-442.

The creation and utilization of metaphors in adjustment counseling for the blind is presented. The author includes metaphorical stories which he utilized as a rehabilitation teacher.

336 Brok, A.J. (1992). Crises and transitions: Gender and life stage issues in individual, group, and couples treatment. Special issue: Psycho-analysis of the mid-life and older patient. Psychoanalysis and Psycho-therapy, 10(1), 3-16.

Three cases are utilized to illustrate important issues that clinicians need to consider when working with middle-aged and older persons in individual, group, and couples therapy. The goal is to assist patients in the transformation of potentially traumatic events into a healthy developmental transition through analytic therapy.

337 Burke, M.J., & Hayes, R.L. (1986). Peer counseling for elderly victims of crime and violence. Journal for Specialists in Group Work, 11(2), 107-113.

Two programs in Illinois are described which are designed to train older persons as volunteers to counsel other older persons in methods of self-protection. Participants report increases in communication skills, knowledge of community services, and problem solving abilities.

338 Burlingame, V.S. (1988). Counseling an older person. Social Casework, 69(9), 588-592.

A case study of an 84-year-old woman is discussed in regards to the difficulty of making a diagnosis for depressed elderly clients. Issues concerning health problems, depression, and a changing self-concept are also reviewed.

339 Clements, J.C. (1984). Older adults: Counseling issues. In brief: An information digest from ERIC/CAPS. Ann Arbor, MI: ERIC/CAPS.

This digest focuses on special concerns of older persons, including employment issues, retirement, problems of aging, and continuing education. Suggestions for how counselors can address these issues are included.

340 Crose, R. (1992). Gerontology is only aging, it's not dead yet. Counseling Psychologist, 20(2), 330-335.

This commentary on Fry's review of social aging theories points out that most citations in the review are more then 10 years old and perpetuate a negative stereotypical image of older persons.

341 Decker, T.W., Cline-Elsen, J., & Gallagher, M. (1992). Relaxation therapy as an adjunct in radiation oncology. Journal of Clinical Psychology, 48(3), 388-393.

The results of a study designed to examine the impact of relaxation therapy, including relaxation training and imagery, on patients undergoing curative and palliative radiotherapy are reported. Results indicate significant reductions in the treatment group in tension, depression, anger, and fatigue. Based on these findings, the study concludes that relaxation therapy appears to improve psychological well-being and quality of life in these patients.

**342   Dettman, D.F. (1992). A clinical reaction to Fry: "Phil is 83..."
        Counseling Psychologist, 20(2), 346-351.**

The case of a recently-widowed 83 year old man living in a geriatric center is
presented as an illustration of how counseling may be tailored to meet the sexual-
social needs of the older individual. The reciprocal influence of individual and
social/family systems is illustrated.

**343   Duffy, M., & Iscoe, I. (1990). Crisis theory and management: The case
        of the older person. Journal of Mental Health Counseling, 12(3), 303-
        313.**

Older persons experience predictable crises in later life, many of which are
serious in nature. Appropriate planning can help to alleviate predictable patterns
of crisis response.

**344   Eisenberg, D.M., & Carilio, T.E. (1990). Friends of the family:
        Counseling elders at family service agencies. Generations, 14(1), 25-26.**

Family service agencies have traditionally been a source of counseling for
individuals, couples, and families in coping with the stresses of life, including
aging. They can be especially important sources of assistance for older persons
living in the community.

**345   Erlanger, M.A. (1990). Using the genogram with the older client.
        Journal of Mental Health Counseling, 12(3), 321-331.**

This article discusses psychological theory and clinical reports which lend support
to the use of genograms in counseling older clients. Case examples are included
to demonstrate how using genograms can promote psychological growth in this
population.

**346   Fry, P.S. (1992). Major social theories of aging and their implications
        for counseling concepts and practice: A critical review. Counseling
        Psychologist, 20(2), 246-329.**

This article provides an extensive review of social theories of aging, including
disengagement, abandonment, activity, role, continuity, liberation and solidarity,
and socioenvironmental theories. It is suggested that counselors can best work
with older people through understanding the synergistic nature of ecological,
biological, psychosocial, and cultural aspects of aging.

**347   Fry, P.S. (1990). The person-environment congruence model:
        Implications and applications for adjustment counseling with older
        adults. Journal for the Advancement of Counseling, 13(2), 87-106.**

This author suggests that negative self-images in later life are the result of failures in life circumstances where environmental influences are overly restrictive, leaving older persons few choices for independent decision making. The person-environment fit model is presented as a basis for counseling with older persons.

348   Gotterer, S.M. (1989). Storytelling: A valuable supplement to poetry writing with the elderly. Arts in Psychotherapy, 16(2), 127-131.

This article describes how the combined use of poetry and storytelling enhanced the therapeutic benefits of each approach for groups of older women living in retirement homes. Both techniques provided opportunities for mental stimulation, expression, and creative growth.

349   Hammarlund, E.R., Ostrom, J.R., & Kethley, A.J. (1985). The effects of drug counseling and other educational strategies on drug utilization in the elderly. Medical Care, 23(2), 165-170.

This article reports the results of a study of medication behavior of older persons living in an apartment complex for older persons. It appears that drug counseling is an effective health promotion strategy in this setting.

350   Johnson, R., Schwiebert, V., & Alvarado, P. (1994). Factors influencing nursing home placement decisions: The older adult's perspective. Clinical Nursing Research, 3(3), 269-281.

This article discusses the results of a research study investigating older adult's perceptions of factors influencing the decision to move to more supportive housing (nursing homes). Results are presented and implications for nursing and counseling interventions discussed.

351   Kosberg, J.I., & Garcia, J.L. (1987). The problems of older clients seen in a family service agency. Journal of Gerontological Social Work, 11(3-4), 141-153.

The authors studied 60 older clients receiving professional counseling services at a family services agency in Florida. Short-term counseling was effective, and many presenting problems could be ameliorated by strengthening interpersonal skills and encouraging self-development.

352   Kunkel, M., & Williams, C. (1991). Age and expectations about counseling: Two methodological perspectives. Journal of Counseling and Development, 70(2), 314-320.

This article describes the results of a study which employed quantitative and phenomenological research methods to examine counseling expectations in older persons. Results indicate differences in expectations of counseling among elderly and younger subjects. Implications for counselors working with older persons are included.

353 McCloskey, L.J. (1990). The silent heart sings. Generations, 14(1), 63-65.

This article describes the development of a program which combines music therapy with life review. The program has been successful with older persons with cognitive impairments and terminal illness.

354 Myers, J.E. (1989). Adult children and aging parents. Alexandria, VA: American Counseling Association.

This book was written for counselors and others working with adult children caring for aging parents. Topics included are normative developmental issues in later life, issues related to aging (depression, suicide, substance abuse), psychosocial concerns of caregivers and adult children, family stress situations, and several counseling interventions.

355 Myers, J.E. (1990). Empowerment for later life. ERIC.

This text hypothesizes that American society unfairly and arbitrarily restricts the opportunities and activities of older persons based purely on their age. The text explores in detail the idea of empowering older persons to overcome the negative effects of societal attitudes by helping the aged gain a sense of power and control in their lives.

356 Nelson, R.C. (1989). Choice awareness: A group experience in a residential setting. Journal for Specialists in Group Work, 14(3), 158-169.

This article describes choice awareness therapy as a group intervention to enable residents to understand their choices and make more effective choices to deal with their life concerns.

357 Osborn, C.L. (1989). Reminiscence: When the past eases the present. Journal of Gerontological Nursing, 15(10), 6-12.

Nurses are encouraged to consider reminiscence groups as an intervention strategy for older adults. Factors critical to the success of groups include defining the purpose, structure, and goals, leadership style, and group process.

358 Pineault, R., Champagne, F., & Maheux, B. (1989). Determinants of health counseling practices in hospitals: The patient's perspective. American Journal of Preventive Medicine, 5(5), 257-265.

This article reports on a study conducted in three hospitals which concluded that persons aged 55-69 were most likely to receive health counseling. They also were more likely to receive treatment in the hospital from a physician other than the one who referred them for treatment.

359 Ponzo, Z. (1992). Promoting successful aging: Problems, opportunities, and counseling guidelines. Journal of Counseling and Development, 71(2), 210-213.

This author recommends that counselors promote successful aging by focusing on wellness strategies before people reach later life. Key areas of intervention are consciousness, control, and change.

360 Robison, F., Smaby, M., & Donovan, G.L. (1989). Influencing reluctant elderly clients to participate in mental health counseling. Journal of Mental Health Co, 11(3), 259-272.

Several interventions are described through which counselors can influence reluctant older clients to participate in counseling. Ethical and evaluation issues related to the use of influence with older persons are discussed.

361 Rybarczyk, B.D., & Auerbach, S.M. (1990). Reminiscence interviews as stress management interventions for older patients undergoing surgery. Gerontologist, 30(4), 522-528.

The authors used reminiscence interviews and interviews focused on successfully met challenges to reduce anxiety and enhance self-perceptions of efficacy in older males facing surgery. Both methods were effective, regardless of whether age-peer or younger age interviewers were used.

362 Schwiebert, V., & Giordano, F. (Spring, 1994). Empowerment: An approach to maintaining dignity and self-esteem throughout the lifespan. Journal of Humanistic Education and Development.

This article discusses the concept of empowerment as an approach to assisting clients in maintaining dignity and self-esteem throughout the lifespan. Implications for counselors working with older persons are discussed.

363 Semel, V. (1990). Confrontation with hopelessness: Psychoanalytic treatment of the older woman. Modern Psychoanalysis, 15(2). 215-224.

This article presents the case study of a 63 year old woman in which feelings of hopelessness are resolved through psychoanalytic treatment. The quality of the therapy was changed when the therapist resolved countertransference issues of hopelessness.

364 Sherman, E. (1987). Reminiscence groups for community elderly. Gerontologist, 27(5), 569-572.

The author compared two types of reminiscence groups: one using a conventional format to recall memories from different life stages and one using an experiential format that focused on feelings and thoughts. All groups reported increases in satisfaction and self-concept.

365   Smyer, M.A. (1984). Life transitions and aging: Implications for counseling older adults. Counseling Psychologist, 12(2), 17-28.

A conceptual framework for counseling older adults and their families is recommended. Counselors need to assist older clients in differentiating normal from abnormal aspects of aging and focus on preventive interventions with older persons and their families.

366   Thompson, J.D., & Scott, N.A. (1991). Counseling service features: Elders' preferences and utilization. Clinical Gerontologist, 11(1), 39-46.

A survey of 84 adults, age 60-93 years old, was conducted to determine the preferences of older persons in regards to desirable features of counseling services. Counseling format and site, as well as counselor age and expertise were some of the features considered by this survey. The study concluded that there was a preference for older-aged, volunteer counselors by the older persons surveyed.

367   Toseland, R.W., & Smith, G.C. (1990). Effectiveness of individual counseling by professional and peer helpers for family caregivers of the elderly. Psychology and Aging, 5(2), 256-263.

Daughters and daughters-in-law who were primary caregivers for frail elderly who received counseling reported significantly higher levels of subjective well being and lower levels psychiatric symptomology than a no-treatment control group. Both peer and professional counseling were provided, with positive but less significant gains for the peer counseling group.

368   Waters, E.B. (1984). Building on what you know: Techniques for individual and group counseling with older people. Counseling Psychologist, 12(2), 63-74.

The author discusses practical aspects of counseling with older persons, noting a variety of similarities and differences in counseling older and younger populations. The value of group work is stressed, and examples of group interventions are provided.

369   Webster, J.D., & Young, R.A. (1988). Process variables of the life review: Counseling implications. International Journal of Aging and Human Development, 26(4), 315-323.

The concept of life review is examined within a developmental framework as a dynamic occurrence in which the individual is an active agent. Possible counseling interventions for older clients are explored.

370   Wellman, F.E., & McCormack, J. (1984). Counseling with older persons: A review of outcome research. Counseling Psychologist, 12(2), 81-96.

The authors conducted an extensive review of outcome research studies on counseling older persons. Interventions which provide a high level of client control rather than passive levels are more effective.

371   White, D., & Ingersoll, D.B. (1989). Life review groups: Helping the member with an unhappy life. Clinical Gerontologist, 8(4), 47-50.

Two cases are presented which demonstrate how life review groups can be adapted to help older people with particularly unhappy lives. It is important for leaders to highlight participants' past accomplishments while allowing them to review selectively past painful events.

372   Woodruff, J.C., Donnan, H., & Halpin, G. (1988). Changing elderly persons' attitudes toward mental health professionals. Gerontologist, 28(6), 800-802.

The authors showed a videotape describing how mental health professionals can help people cope with problems to 56 workers in senior companion and foster grandparent programs. Subjects were more disposed to receiving counseling after viewing the program than were members of a matched control group.

LIFE REVIEW

373   Crose, R. (1990). Reviewing the past in the here and now: Using Gestalt therapy techniques with life review. Journal of Mental Health Counseling, 12(3), 279-287.

The author presents a Gestalt therapy perspective on the life review process and discusses the use of Gestalt techniques in helping older clients achieve resolution of past conflicts. Case examples are used the illustrate the techniques.

374   Hughston, G.A., & Cooledge, N.J. (1989). The life review: An underutilized strategy for systemic family intervention. Journal of Psychotherapy and the Family, 5(1-2), 47-55.

The authors describe life review as an underutilized strategy for intervention with older persons and their families. Benefits for both therapists and clients are enumerated, including the importance of understanding the past in avoidance of repeated mistakes.

375   Magee, J.J. (1991). Dream analysis as an aid to older adults' life review. Journal of Gerontological Social Work, 18(1-2), 163-173.

The introduction of dream analysis into groups of older persons already involved in the life review process is presented. A model of dream analysis is discussed in this article, as is the background in dream analysis that social workers need, and the benefit of dream analysis for the older person.

376   Malde, S. (1988). Guided autobiography: A counseling tool for older adults. Journal of Counseling and Development, 66(6), 290-292.

Thirty-nine community volunteers participated in a study to determine the usefulness of an educational-counseling course based on life review in helping older persons face critical life challenges. Informal evaluations were positive, however statistical tests did not produce significant results.

377   Osborn, C.L. (1989). Reminiscence: When the past eases the present. Journal of Gerontological Nursing, 15(10), 6-12.

Nurses are encouraged to consider reminiscence groups as an intervention strategy for older adults. Factors critical to the success of groups include defining the purpose, structure, and goals, leadership style, and group process.

378   Rybarczyk, B.D., & Auerbach, S.M. (1990). Reminiscence interviews as stress management interventions for older patients undergoing surgery. Gerontologist, 30(4), 522-528.

The authors used reminiscence interviews and interviews focused on successfully met challenges to reduce anxiety and enhance self-perceptions of efficacy in older males facing surgery. Both methods were effective, regardless of whether age-peer or younger age interviewers were used.

379   Webster, J.D., & Young, R.A. (1988). Process variables of the life review: Counseling implications. International Journal of Aging and Human Development, 26(4), 315-323.

The concept of life review is examined within a developmental framework as a dynamic occurrence in which the individual is an active agent. Possible counseling interventions for older clients are explored.

380   White, D., & Ingersoll, D.B. (1989). Life review groups: Helping the member with an unhappy life. Clinical Gerontologist, 8(4), 47-50.

Two cases are presented which demonstrate how life review groups can be adapted to help older people with particularly unhappy lives. It is important for leaders to highlight participants' past accomplishments while allowing them to review selectively past painful events.

381   Youssef, F.A. (1990). The impact of group reminiscence counseling on a depressed elderly population. Nurse Practitioner: American Journal of Primary Health Care, 15(4), 32-38.

The goal of this study was to determine the effect of group reminiscence counseling on the level of depression of older women living in a nursing home. Sixty women, age 65 and older, were randomly divided into a control group and two experimental groups. Data was collected using Beck's Depression Inventory and demographic data. The results of the study imply that group reminiscence counseling did have an effect on the level of depression of the elderly women.

382   Randall, R.L. (1986). Reminiscing in the elderly: Pastoral care of self-narratives. Journal of Pastoral Care, 40(3), 207-215.

The role of reminiscence in older persons is discussed from the perspective of self-psychology. Aging places stress on the self-system and restoration of the strength of this system is essential in counseling.

383   Singer, V.I., Tracz, S.M., & Dworkin, S.H. (1991). Reminiscence group therapy: A treatment modality for older adults. Journal for Specialist's in Group Work, 16(3), 167-171.

This article describes a reminiscence group therapy program in an adult day care center. Participants became increasingly talkative over time, developed group cohesion, and experienced decreased depression.

INTEGRATIVE COUNSELING

384   Glass, J.C., & Grant, K.A. (1983). Counseling in the later years: A growing need. Personnel and Guidance Journal, 62(4), 210-213.

Transitions of aging are discussed, as are the factors which influence one's ability to cope with these changes. This article also presents suggestions for meeting the needs of the elderly person in their struggle to cope with transitions and losses.

385   Ramamurti, P.V., Jamuna, D., & Reddy, L.K. (1992). Improving human resources among the elderly: Effect of an intervention. Journal of Personality and Clinical Studies, 8(1-2), 77-79.

Twenty urban retired men participated in an intervention program which enhanced markers of successful aging in five areas: self-acceptance of aging changes, self-perception of health, activities of daily living, familial and social relationships, and flexibility of behavior.

FAMILY AND GROUP COUNSELING

386   Allred, G.B., & Dobson, J.E. (1987). Remotivation group
        interactions: Increasing children's contact with the elderly.
        Elementary School Guidance and Counseling, 21(3), 216-220.

Small, positive shifts in children's attitudes occurred following participation in an
intergenerational remotivation therapy program. Written evaluations indicated that
many children gained new perceptions of older adults.

387   Burlew, L.D., Jones, J., & Emerson, P. (1991). Exercise and the
        elderly: A group counseling approach. Journal for Specialist's in
        Group Work, 16(3), 152-158.

Group counseling is presented as a means of enhancing exercise participation and
compliance among older adults. Daily exercise is encouraged as a means of
improving both physiological and psychological functioning.

388   Capuzzi, D. (1990). Recent trends in group work with the elderly.
        Generations, 14(1), 43-48.

The author summarizes the major categories of group work with older persons,
including approaches designed for both cognitively impaired and well elderly.
Considerations for adapting groups to the needs of older individuals are provided.

389   Capuzzi, D., & Gossman, L. (1982). Sexuality and the elderly: A
        group counseling model. Journal for Specialists in Group Work,
        7(4), 251-259.

This article provides a description of a group counseling model designed to
facilitate the exploration of the issues of sexuality for older adults. The article
includes information pertaining to issues such as member selection, leadership
style, and length and setting of the group.

390   Cohen, P.M. (1983). A group approach for working with families of
        the elderly. Gerontologist, 23(3), 248-250.

A group approach was utilized for the support and sharing of family members
caring for elderly persons. The group process was beneficial to family members
in resolving problems associated with caring for an elderly relative.

391   Cox, C., & Ephross, P.H. (1989). Group work with families of
        nursing home residents: Its socialization and therapeutic functions.
        Journal of Gerontological Social Work, 13(3-4), 61-73.

Group interventions with families of nursing home residents permit family
members to express and deal with negative emotions that often accompany

placement of an older relative. Guilt and stress are reduced, and new roles and behaviors appropriate to the institution may be learned.

392   Dracup, K., Meleis, A.I., Clark, S., Clyburn, A., Shields, L., & Staley, M. (1984). Group counseling in cardiac rehabilitation: effect on patient compliance. Patient Education and Counseling, 6(4), 169-177.

This study examines the effects of group counseling as a strategy for increasing patient compliance in a cardiac patient population.

393   Florsheim, M.J., & Herr, J.J. (1990). Family counseling with elders: A useful and positive starting point. Generations, 14(1), 40-42.

This article discusses the strengths and weaknesses of family counseling with an elderly person, and provides a description of the process. Many related issues are also addressed.

394   Genevay, D. (1990). The aging-family consultation: A "summit conference" model of brief therapy. Generations, 14(1),58-60.

An aging-family consultation model is presented which enables multigenerational families to begin coping with their real needs and dilemmas. Intensive brief therapy is recommended.

395   Gorey, K.M., & Cryns, A.G. (1991). Group work as interventive modality with older depressed clients. Journal of Gerontological Social Work, 16(1-2), 137-157.

This article reviews 19 empirical studies on group work with older depressed clients; concluding that groups are optimally effective with older clients who live alone and are moderately to severely depressed. Small client groups and brief interventions were most effective.

396   Hargrave, T.D., & Anderson, W. (1990). Helping older people finish well: A contextual family therapy approach. Family Therapy, 17(1), 9-19.

This article describes two case examples of families with a troubled older adult which received counseling over a two year period. Effective family functioning increased with the intergenerational interventions provided.

397   Hinkle, S.J. (1991). Support group counseling for caregivers of Alzheimer's disease patients. Journal for Specialist's in Group Work, 16(3), 185-190.

This article presents information concerning Alzheimer's disease and the effectiveness of support groups for caregivers of Alzheimer's disease patients.

Supportive counseling is seen as helpful in addressing the concerns of caregivers and specific family issues.

398   Hittner, A., & Bornstein, H. (1990). Group counseling with older adults: Coping with late-onset hearing impairment. Journal of Mental Health Counseling, 12(3), 332-341.

Counselors working with older adults should expect that 25% of their clients will experience hearing difficulties. Suggestions for modifying group counseling interventions to accommodate the needs of older hearing impaired clients are provided.

399   Johnson, W.Y., & Wilborn, B. (1991). Group counseling as an intervention in anger expression and depression in older adults. Journal for Specialist's in Group Work, 16(3), 133-142.

The link between anger and depression was examined through an anger awareness group with older women. Though no change in awareness or expression of anger occurred, self-reports of the group experience were positive.

400   McDaniel, B.A. (1989). A group work experience with mentally retarded adults on the issues of death and dying. Journal of Gerontological Social Work, 13(3-4), 187-191.

A support group for eight older adults with mild mental retardation is described. The group focused on death and dying, with positive benefits for participants.

401   Morse, R.L. (1989). Roles of the psychotherapist in family financial counseling: A systems approach to prolongation of independence. Journal of Psychotherapy and the Family, 5(1-2), 133-147.

The author suggests that therapists can assist clients in integrating good health, feelings of self-worth, and a sense of economic security to enhance their independent living in later life. A systems approach to developing factual client profiles on which to base interventions is described.

402   Myers, J.E., Poidevant, J.P., & Dean, L. (1991). Groups for older persons and their caregivers: A review of the literature. Journal for Specialist's in Group Work, 16(3), 197-205.

This article presents a review of the literature on group interventions with older disabled persons and their caregivers. Groups are most successful when participants are carefully selected, counselors have adequate knowledge of the needs of their clients, and attempts are made to accommodate for client needs.

403   Nelson, R.C. (1989). Choice awareness: A group experience in a residential setting. Journal for Specialists in Group Work, 14(3), 158-169.

This article describes choice awareness therapy as a group intervention to enable residents to understand their choices and make more effective choices to deal with their life concerns.

404   Osborn, C.L. (1989). Reminiscence: When the past eases the present. Journal of Gerontological Nursing, 15(10), 6-12.

Nurses are encouraged to consider reminiscence groups as an intervention strategy for older adults. Factors critical to the success of groups include defining the purpose, structure, and goals, leadership style, and group process.

405   Scharlach, A.E. (1989). Social group work with the elderly: A role theory perspective. Social Work With Groups, 12(3), 33-46.

This article illustrates how role theory can be applied in social group work with older adults. Role transitions in later life require particular attention as older persons often benefit from assistance with the psychosocial challenges these transitions impose.

406   Schwartzben, S.H. (1989). The 10th floor family support group: A descriptive model of the use of a multi-family group in a home for the aged. Social Work With Groups, 12(1), 41-54.

This article describes an effective multifamily group experience in an institutional setting. The families were mutually supportive and were able to effect interventions in the setting on behalf of residents.

407   Stone, M.L., & Waters, E. (1991). Accentuate the positive: A peer group counseling program for older adults. Special issue: Group work with the aging and their caregivers. Journal for Specialists in Group Work, 16(3), 159-166.

A group therapy program designed to reduce stress in adults age 55 and over is discussed. The primary focuses of the program are: 1) developing skills for identifying stress; 2) increasing self-esteem; and 3) developing skills for coping with stress. The role of peer counselors in this setting is also described.

408   Szwabo, P., & Thale, T.T. (1983, November). Expressive group psychotherapy with the older adult. Paper presented at the Annual Scientific Meeting of the Gerontological Society, San Francisco, CA.

This paper reports on a psycho-dynamically oriented group of 6 elderly adults to determine the usefulness of this approach with the older adult population. Insight-oriented techniques, as well as support and socialization strategies, were utilized to explore issues such as depression, death, loneliness, and health problems related to the process of aging. This type of group therapy was shown to be beneficial for older adults.

409   Thomas, M.C., & Martin, V. (1992). Training counselors to facilitate the transitions of aging through group work. Counselor Education and Supervision, 32(1), 51-60.

Literature on group work with older persons is reviewed. Group work is discussed as an effective intervention with this population; however, counselor educators need to provide specialized training of facilitators if groups are to be successful.

410   Toseland, R.M., Rossiter, C.M., & Labrecque, M.S. (1989), The effectiveness of three group intervention strategies to support family caregivers. American Journal of Orthopsychiatry, 59(3), 420-429.

In the study described in this article, both peer and professional leaders helped caregivers cope with the stress of caring for a frail parent. Caregivers reported many positive changes from their participation in the 8-week group sessions, but did not report any reductions in perceived burden.

411   Waters, E.B. (1984). Building on what you know: Techniques for individual and group counseling with older people. Counseling Psychologist, 12(2), 63-74.

The author discusses practical aspects of counseling with older persons, noting a variety of similarities and differences in counseling older and younger populations. The value of group work is stressed, and examples of group interventions are provided.

412   Weisman, C.B., & Schwartz, P. (1989). Worker expectations in group work with the frail elderly: Modifying the models for a better fit. Social Work With Groups, 12(3), 47-55.

The frail elderly are defined as a population different from other older persons in that they have significant dependence on others and social-emotional, physical and/or mental impairment. Modifications of traditional social group work practice is required to meet their needs effectively.

413   White, D., & Ingersoll, D.B. (1989). Life review groups: Helping the member with an unhappy life. Clinical Gerontologist, 8(4), 47-50.

Two cases are presented which demonstrate how life review groups can be adapted to help older people with particularly unhappy lives. It is important for leaders to highlight participants' past accomplishments while allowing them to review selectively past painful events.

414   Youssef, F.A. (1990). The impact of group reminiscence counseling on a depressed elderly population. Nurse Practitioner: American Journal of Primary Health Care, 15(4), 32-38.

The goal of this study was to determine the effect of group reminiscence counseling on the level of depression of older women living in a nursing home. Sixty women, age 65 and older, were randomly divided into a control group and two experimental groups. Data was collected using Beck's Depression Inventory and demographic data. The results of the study imply that group reminiscence counseling did have an effect on the level of depression of the elderly women.

415   Zimpfer, D. (1987). Groups for the aging. Journal for Specialists in Group Work, 12(2), 85-92.

This article reviews 19 studies to determine the effectiveness of group counseling with older persons. Several conclusions are presented to enhance group interventions with this population.

PARAPROFESSIONAL AND PEER COUNSELING

416   Bratter, B., & Freeman, E. (1990). The maturing of peer counseling. Generations, 14(1), 49-52.

A 12-week, 24-session program of peer counseling training is presented which emphasized the significance of client-counselor bonding and personal growth. Central attention in training is given to identifying the goals of the client.

417   Burke, M.J., & Hayes, R.L. (1986). Peer counseling for elderly victims of crime and violence. Journal for Specialists in Group Work, 11(2), 107-113.

Two programs in Illinois are described which are designed to train older persons as volunteers to counsel other older persons in methods of self-protection. Participants report increases in communication skills, knowledge of community services, and problem solving abilities.

418   Crose, R., Duffy, M., Warren, J., & Franklin, B. (1987). Project OASIS: Volunteer mental health paraprofessional serving nursing home residents. Gerontologist, 27(3), 359-362.

A 2-year model demonstration project designed to train adult volunteers in the delivery of mental health services to older persons is described. Topics discussed included volunteer recruitment, training, and supervision, and program outcomes.

**419   De-Vries, B., & Petty, B.J. (1992). Peer-counseling training: Analysis
         of personal growth for older adults. Educational Gerontology, 18(4),
         381-393.**

This study compared differences between and within two groups of elderly adults.
One group completed a 12-month peer-counseling training program, and the other
was a comparison group. The results showed that overall life satisfaction
significantly increased for the members of the peer-counseling training program
during the 12 months of the program.

**420   Fling, S., & Taylor, B. (1983, April). A visitation/training program
         for institutionalized elderly. Paper presented at the Annual
         Convention of the Southwestern Psychological Association, San
         Antonio, TX.**

The effects of a visitation program on 25 nursing home residents and on the
college students and elderly persons who made visits were studied. The results
showed a significant correlation between the resident's level of self-esteem and
the level of counseling skills of the visitor. The college student visitors
demonstrated a significant improvement in their counseling skills, knowledge and
attitudes related to aging.

**421   Folken, M.H. (1991). The importance of group support for widowed
         persons. Journal for Specialist's in Group Work, 16(3), 172-177.**

The Widowed Persons Service, a national program developed to meet the needs
of newly widowed persons, is described. Trained paraprofessional counselors,
persons who themselves have made a satisfactory adjustment to their own loss
of a spouse, are the service providers for the program..

**422   France, M.H. (1989). Residents helpers: Peer counseling in a long
         term care facility. Canadian Journal of Counselling, 23(1), 113-119.**

This article describes a peer counseling program in a 300 bed long term care
facility in British Columbia. An outline of the training program and comments
from participants and staff are included in the report.

**423   Glanz, K., Marger, S.M., & Meehan, E.F. (1986). Evaluation of a
         peer educator stroke education program for the elderly. Health
         Education Research, 1(2), 121-130.**

The authors conducted both process and outcome studies of a stroke risk factor
education program which used elderly peer facilitators. The program was
successful in training effective peer facilitators.

424   Lynde, B.D. (1992). Nutrition promotion: A case study in peer education. Journal of Nutrition for the Community Psychology, 16(4), 428-436.

The peer education model was tested in this study. Counselors were successful in addressing a wide range of caller concerns. Reasons for the success and benefits of the peer education model are discussed.

425   Nagel, J. (1988). Efficacy of elderly and adolescent volunteer counselors in a nursing home setting. Journal of Counseling Psychology, 35(1), 81-86.

Elderly and adolescent volunteer counselors met twice a week with nursing home residents for five weeks. The level of depression improved in nursing home residents who saw a volunteer counselor. The study did not find the method of training, or the age of the volunteer to be significant.

426   Petty, B.J., & Cusack, S.A. (1989). Assessing the impact of a senior's peer counseling program. Educational Gerontology, 15(1), 49-64.

This article describes an 18-month program for peer counseling training conducted in Canada. The program was effective in enabling seniors to take a more active role in their community support network.

427   Rose, M.A. (1992). Evaluation of a peer-education program on heart disease prevention with older adults. Public Health Nursing, 9(4), 242-247.

The results of a cardiovascular disease peer education program are discussed. The study found statistically significant increases in several areas, including the participant's general knowledge of heart disease.

428   Smith, M.F., Tobin, S.S., & Toseland, R.W. (1992). Therapeutic processes in professional and peer counseling of family caregivers of frail elderly people. Social Work, 37(4), 345-351.

A study comparing the therapeutic processes utilized by peer counselors and professional counselors when counseling caretakers of the elderly is discussed. The study found that professional counselors tended to be friendlier and more willing to give advice than peer counselors.

429   Stone, M.L., & Waters, E. (1991). Accentuate the positive: A peer group counseling program for older adults. Special issue: Group work with the aging and their caregivers. Journal for Specialists in Group Work, 16(3), 159-166.

A group therapy program designed to reduce stress in adults age 55 and over is discussed. The primary focuses of the program are: 1) developing skills for identifying stress; 2) increasing self-esteem; and 3) developing skills for coping with stress. The role of peer counselors in this setting is also described.

430   Toseland, R.W., & Smith, G.C. (1990). Effectiveness of individual counseling by professional and peer helpers for family caregivers of the elderly. Psychology and Aging, 5(2), 256-263.

Daughters and daughters-in-law who were primary caregivers for frail elderly who received counseling reported significantly higher levels of subjective well being and lower levels psychiatric symptomology than a no-treatment control group. Both peer and professional counseling were provided, with positive but less significant gains for the peer counseling group.

SELF-HELP GROUPS

431   Redburn, D.E., & Juretich, M. (1989). Some considerations for using widowed self-help group leaders. Gerontology and Geriatrics Education, 9(3), 89-98.

Peer leaders have great potential for helping other older persons who have had recent similar experiences. However, professionals must be sensitive to their needs for counseling related to issues such as grief, depression, self-esteem, life satisfaction, and loneliness.

432   Reever, K.E., & Thomas, E. (1985). Training facilitators of self-help groups for caregivers to elders. Generations, 10(1), 50-52.

This article discusses self-help and caregiving concerns which should be addressed in training peer helpers. Topics included are sharing of leadership, types of facilitators, and areas for training.

433   Schwiebert, V., & Myers, J.E. (July/August, 1994). A psycho-educational counseling intervention for midlife adult children with parent-care responsibilities. Journal of Counseling and Development.

This article presents the results of a study of the effectiveness of a psycho-educational counseling intervention for midlife adult children caring for aging parents. The intervention is described, results discussed, and implications for counseling included.

434   Stone, I., & Koonin, M. (1986). A support group in a retirement home. Aging, 352, 18-19.

The formation and progress of a support group of older persons in a church-supported retirement facility is described. A variety of issues surfaced during the eight week program, including fear, anger, frustration, and loss.

435   Toseland, R.W., Rossiter, C.M., Oeak, T., & Hill, P. (1990). Therapeutic processes in peer led and professionally led support groups for caregivers. International Journal of Group Psychotherapy, 40(3), 279-303.

Peer and professionally led support groups for caregivers of frail older persons were compared. Both groups were effective in helping caregivers ventilate negative emotions and experience support and sharing.

436   Zimmer, A.H. (1987-88). Self-help groups & late-life learning. Generations, 12(2), 19-21.

Generally self-help groups assume that the individuals participating in the group have the ability to overcome their problems, and that the participants have needs that are not being satisfied. The value of self-help groups for older persons coping with typical concerns is discussed.

CREATIVE ART THERAPIES: POETRY, WRITING, DRAMA

437   Edwards, M. (1990). Poetry: Vehicle for retrospection and delight. Generations, 14(1), 61-62.

The author describes the use of a poetry group in a long term care facility as a means of stimulating cognition, life review, and resolution of unresolved conflicts. Poetry also inspired creativity among the older participants.

438   Gotterer, S.M. (1989). Storytelling: A valuable supplement to poetry writing with the elderly. Arts in Psychotherapy, 16(2), 127-131.

This article describes how the combined use of poetry and storytelling enhanced the therapeutic benefits of each approach for groups of older women living in retirement homes. Both techniques provided opportunities for mental stimulation, expression, and creative growth.

BIBLIOTHERAPY

439   Hynes, A.L., & Wedl, L.C. (1990). Bibliotherapy: An interactive process in counseling older persons. Journal of Mental Health Counseling, 12(3), 288-302.

These authors describe the interactive process of bibliotherapy as a means of helping older persons explore both cognitive and emotional reactions and experiences. Media used may be books, poetry, or any of a variety of creative arts.

MUSIC, MOVEMENT, AND DANCE THERAPIES

440   Barke, C.R., & Nicholas, D.R. (1990). Physical activity in older adults: The stages of change. Journal of Applied Gerontology, 9(2), 216-223.

Stages of change among older adults were measured and compared across groups. Exercise and Elderhostel groups scored higher on action and maintenance of activities than retirees who did not participate in either program.

REALITY ORIENTATION, REMOTIVATION, RESOCIALIZATION

441   Brammer, L.M. (1985). Counseling and quality of life for older adults: Beating the odds. Educational Perspectives, 23(3), 13-16.

Counseling strategies which are utilized to help older adults take control of their lives ar discussed. These strategies are presented in the context of enhancing an individual's quality of life.

442   McCrone, S.H. (1991). Resocialization group treatment with the confused institutionalized elderly. Western Journal of Nursing Research, 13(1), 30-45.

A study of 80 nursing home residents demonstrates the positive results that can be achieved through small group treatment. The article concludes with two commentaries on the study and McCrone's response.

6

Ethics in Gerontological Counseling

443   Agresti, A.A. (1992). Counselor training and ethical issues with
       older clients. Special section: Training in gerontological counseling.
       Counselor Education and Supervision, 32(1), 43-50.

A training program for teaching ethics in counseling programs designed to
prepare professionals to work with the aged is discussed. Both the rationale for
incorporating such ethics training into current programs, and suggestions for
integrating such training into these programs are explored.

444   Burr, H.T. (1985, November). Clinical aspects of assessment and
       intervention with resistant clients. Paper presented at the Annual
       Scientific Meeting of the Gerontological Society, New Orleans, LA.

The difficulties presented by an aged patient who is resistant to treatment are
considered. The elderly individual may view suggestions and assistance as
attempts to compromise their individual autonomy.

445   Cavallaro, M.L., & Ramsey, M. (1988). Ethical issues in
       gerocounseling. Counseling and Values, 32(3), 221-227.

The authors discuss ethical issues in gerocounseling and explore how these issues
affect the counseling relationship with older clients. It is important to assess the
cognitive capacity of older clients, particularly when the counselor is retained by
a third party to assist the older individual.

446   Fitting, M.D. (1984). Professional and ethical responsibilities for
       psychologists working with the elderly. Counseling Psychologist,
       12(2), 69-78.

Differential diagnosis of functional versus organic etiology may be difficult when working with older persons, but is essential because treatment decisions must be based on the diagnosis.

447   Janocko, K.M., & Lee, S.S. (1988). Ethical implications of de-institutionalization and moves of the institutionalized elderly. Professional Psychology Research and practice, 19(5), 522-526.

Awareness of the long-term effects of institutionalization and the effects of relocation on older persons create ethical conflicts for psychologists involved in discharge planning in institutional settings.

448   Myers, J.E. (1990). Aging: An overview for mental health counselors. Journal of Mental Health Counseling, 12(3), 245-259.

Issues in regards to counseling elderly persons are discussed, including countertransference. The importance of outcome research in relation to counseling the elderly is also emphasized.

7

Practica and Internships

449 Cavallaro, M.L. (1990, March). <u>Counseling older women: Curriculum guidelines and strategies</u>. Paper presented at the Annual Meeting of the American Association for Counseling and Development, Cincinnati, OH.

The curriculum for educating counselors needs to include topics related to older women since the geriatric population is predominantly female. This paper discusses the newly adopted standards of the American Association for Counseling and Development in regards to gerontological counseling.

450 Cavallaro, M. (1991). Curriculum guidelines and strategies on counseling older women for incorporation into gerontology and counseling coursework. Special Issue: Women, education, and aging. <u>Educational Gerontology</u>, <u>17</u>(2), 157-166.

This article includes a discussion of several topics which should be incorporated into curriculum in gerontology and counseling. Topics which are discussed include health, physiological changes, osteoporosis, mental health, changes in family relationships, sexuality, substance abuse, and resources.

451 Cox, C. (1983, November). <u>Gerontology education: The needs of local agencies</u>. Paper presented at the Annual Scientific Meeting of the Gerontological Society, San Francisco, CA.

In California, directors of 60 agencies which serve an elderly population were surveyed to determine the needs of an agency in terms of counselor education. The paper outlines the particular areas in which counselors should have knowledge and skill, and compared these qualities to current requirements of gerontology programs.

452   Ganikos, M.L., & Blake, R. (1984). Counseling psychology and aging. Counseling Psychologist, 12(2), 17-99.

This is a composition of eight articles which address many ways in which the field of counseling psychology is meeting the needs of the elderly population. Some of the topics examined include counseling programs, techniques, and theory.

453   Okun, M.A., Stock, W.A., & Weir, R.M. (1985). Doctoral training in the psychology of adult development and aging. Educational Gerontology, 11(4-6), 349-361.

Findings of a study of 361 psychology doctoral training units in the United States reveal that there has been a clear increase in the number of academic units which offer specializations in adult development and aging between 1975 and 1984. Academic units are encouraged to continue adding coursework in this area.

454   Rich, T.A. (1986). Career preparation: A curriculum in mental health and aging for service providers. Final Report. Document.

This is a final report which presents the details of a graduate level curriculum in mental health and aging. The 10 courses of the curriculum are discussed thoroughly, as well as other information pertinent to the development of the program.

455   Rich, T.A., Pinkard, T.A., Dunn, V.K., & Dupree, L.W. (1985). The development of a mental health and aging curriculum. Journal of Applied Gerontology, 4(2), 117-122.

The development and evaluation of a graduate curriculum in mental health and aging is described, including a discussion of issues related to recruitment of students, placement in practica and internship sites, and licensure.

456   Thomas, M.C., & Martin, V. (1992). Training counselors to facilitate the transitions of aging through group work. Special section: Training in gerontological counseling. Counselor Education and Supervision, 32(1), 51-60.

The need for counselors trained in group work with the elderly is indicated. The specific knowledge and skills needed by these counselors is presented.

457   Wilbur, K.H., & Zarit, S.H. (1987). Practicum training in gerontological counseling. Educational Gerontology, 13(1). 15-32.

The elements of a clinical practicum in mental health and aging for both master's and doctoral level students is presented. Supervision, the placement process, and procedural issues are discussed.

RATIONALE FOR PRACTICA AND INTERNSHIPS IN GERONTO-LOGICAL COUNSELING

458   **Coffman, S.L., & Coffman, V.T. (1986). Aging awareness training for professionals who work with the elderly. Small Group Behavior, 17(1), 95-103.**

A workshop designed to create an atmosphere which enables professionals working with the aged to safely and honestly examine various aspects of their profession is presented. Several topics related to working with older persons are discussed.

459   **Eisler, T.A., Hughston, G.A., & Lopez, M. (1985). Training clergy to help the elderly and their families. Journal of Applied Gerontology, 4(2), 58-62.**

This article describes the development, implementation, and evaluation of a training program to increase knowledge of concerns of older persons among clergy. Most subjects perceived the workshops as useful and increased their knowledge of how to best serve the older population.

460   **Myers, J.E. (1991). Trends in gerontological counselor preparation. Counselor Education and Supervision, 30(3), 194-204.**

An examination of the results of a survey of 237 counseling program departments is conducted. The survey notes several trends with respect to programs which prepare counselors to work with the aged.

461   **Larrabee, M.J. (1983). Using simulations to foster understanding of aging. School Counselor, 30(4), 261-268.**

Resource materials to assist school counselors in creating and organizing guidance strategies for educating students with respect to attitudes on aging are discussed. The use of simulation activities for use in the classroom is also presented.

462   **Schlossberg, N.K. (1990). Training counselors to work with older adults. Generations, 14(1), 7-10.**

The training of individuals who wish to counsel adults involves several key elements which are presented and discussed.

463   **Thomas, M.C., & Martin, V. (1992). Training counselors to facilitate the transitions of aging through group work. Counselor Education and Supervision, 32(1), 51-60.**

Group counseling for the aged and the caregivers of the aged is a successful tool in treating these individuals. The resources and needs of counseling training programs are discussed in this regard.

464   Tomine, S. (1986). Private practice in gerontological counseling. Journal of Counseling & Development, 64(6), 406-409.

Various strategies for counseling the aged in a private practice setting are set forth and discussed. A service delivery system and a model are proposed for closing the gap between needs and treatment.

AGENCIES WHERE STUDENTS CAN GAIN INVOLVEMENT WORKING WITH OLDER PEOPLE

465   Peterson, D.A., & Wendt, P.F. (1990). Employment in the field of aging: A survey of professionals in four fields. Gerontologist, 30(5), 679-684.

The results of a survey of members of various professional associations working with older persons are discussed. The survey suggests that the characteristics, education, and perception of professionals working with the aged had changed significantly over the last two decades.

8

The Professional Gerontological Counselor

466   Bernstein, L.O. (1990). A special service: Counseling the individual elderly client. <u>Generations,</u> <u>14</u>(1), 35-38.

Older persons can benefit from counseling, though a slower pace and some modifications of counseling practice may be required. Successful gerontological counselors are those who use a broad range of treatment techniques, and who recognize that education, advocacy, and support are needed, in addition to traditional psychological interventions.

467   Cohen, G. (1984). Counseling interventions for the late twentieth century elderly. <u>Counseling Psychologist,</u> <u>12</u>(2), 97-99.

The current status and future of counseling services for older persons are discussed. Service delivery issues and the question of drug treatments and/or counseling are considered.

468   Leviton, D., & Campanelli, L. (1984). Have we avoided the frail aged and dying older person in HPERD? <u>Health Education,</u> <u>15</u>(6), 43-47.

This article discusses the lack of attention the fields of health, physical education, recreation, and dance have paid to older persons. A model for improved quality of life in this population is presented.

469   Myers, J.E. (1992). Aging: An overview for mental health counselors. <u>Journal of Mental Health Counseling,</u> <u>12</u>(2), 245-259.

This article provides an overview of the relationship between mental health and aging, including similarities and differences in counseling older and younger persons. The social breakdown model is presented and discussed as a basis for planning and implementing interventions with older persons.

470   Myers, J.E., & Rimmer, S. (1982). Assessment of older persons. Measurement and Evaluation in Guidance, 15(3), 182-248.

This edition contains eight articles which explore the area of assessment in the elderly population. Assessment instruments for the geriatric population are reviewed including life satisfaction, attitudes, retirement maturity, and leisure instruments.

471   Qualls, S.H. (1992). Social gerontology theory is not enough: Strategies and resources for counselors. Counseling Psychologist, 20(2), 341-345.

This commentary on Fry's review of social aging theories notes that these theories are only a small part of what counselors need to know to work effectively with older clients.

472   Schlossberg, N.K. (1990). Training counselors to work with older adults. Generations, 14(1), 7-10.

Counselors who work with older adults need special training to help them master changes in their lives. Such training includes perspectives on life transitions and life events and teaching people to cope with changes experienced in later life.

473   Smyer, M.A., & Intrieri, R.C. (1990). Evaluating counseling outcomes. Generations, 14(1), 11-14.

Research on counseling outcomes with older persons is reviewed. Effective counseling requires an understanding of the processes of aging, counseling, and evaluation.

9

Pharmacology and Aging

474 Fincham, J.E. (1986). **Over-the-counter drug use and misuse by the ambulatory elderly.** Journal of Geriatric Drug Therapy, 1(2), 3-21.

The literature on over the counter drug use among older persons is reviewed. Improved counseling and educational strategies are recommended to overcome existing problems in self-medication administration.

475 Kimberlin, C.L., Berardo, D.H., Pendergast, J.F., & McKenzie, L.C. (1993). Med-Care, 31(5), 451-468.

This study discusses the role of the pharmacist in preventing and resolving drug-related problems in patients, particularly in the elderly population. Additionally, the article describes a program designed to teach community pharmacists a process for assessing drug therapy of older clients and a process for intervening to correct problems associated with drug therapy.

476 Koenig, H.G., & Breitner, J.C. (1990). **Use of antidepressants in medically ill older patients.** Psychosomatics, 31(1), 22-32.

This article examines the course of major depression in older patients and its effects on the treatment, course, and outcome of physical illness. Counseling is recommended for persons experiencing depression regardless of whether antidepressants are prescribed as many causes of depression are situational in nature.

477 Mallet, L. (1992). **Counseling in special populations: The elderly population.** American Pharmacist, NS32(10), 71-80.

This article discusses the special counseling needs of the elderly population as related to the practice of pharmacology. Interventions designed for pharmacist use are discussed.

478   Raynor, D., Booth, T., & Blenkinsopp, A. (1993). Effects of computer generated reminder charts on patients' compliance with drug regimens. British Medical Journal, 306(6886), 1158-1161.

This article reports the findings of a study designed to investigate the effects of a reminder chart on patient drug compliance. Results support the use of automatically generated reminder charts to aid in patient drug compliance.

479   Tett, S., Higgins, G., & Armour, C. (1993). Impact of pharmacist interventions on medication management by the elderly: A review of the literature. Pharmacotherapy, 27(1), 80-86.

This study reports the results of a qualitative review of pharmacist interventions as reported in the literture between 1975 and 1990. Results indicate a lack of published evaluations of pharmacist interventions in medication management by older persons.

480   Wolf, K., Gisele, P., Levy, A., Siverstone, F., & Smith, H. (1989). Psychiatric profile of the noncompliant geriatric patient in the community. International Psychogeriatrics, 1(2), 177-184.

This article describes a study of medication compliance in the geriatric population. In addition, a treatment intervention involving weekly pharmacist counseling sessions was instituted. Profiles of non-compliant patients were developed and included three components: absence of family support, mistrust of medical support, and psychiatric illness or personality disorder.

481   Wolfe, S.C., & Schirm, V. (1992). Medication counseling for the elderly: Effects on knowledge and compliance after hospital discharge. Geriatric Nursing New York, 13(3), 134-138.

This study reports both qualitative and quantitative data which add to the nurse's understanding of medication knowledge and compliance in the elderly population. As elderly patients continue to assume more responsibility for self-care, it is essential for healthcare professionals to explore strategies for promoting self-care skills and well-being in this population.

Author Index

Authors are listed by page number, not annotation number.

Subject Index

About the Compilers

VALERIE L. SCHWIEBERT, Assistant Professor of the Gerontology Faculty Association in the Department of Educational Psychology, Counseling, and Special Education at Northern Illinois University, is also certified nationally as a gerontological and rehabilitation counselor. She is president of the Illinois Association for Measurement and Evaluation in Counseling and Development and has contributed to a number of professional journals.

JANE E. MYERS, Professor of Counseling Education at the University of North Carolina at Greensboro, is certified nationally as a gerontological, clinical, and rehabilitation counselor and has received three national awards for her research in gerontology. Among her numerous publications in the field is a three-volume guide, *Counseling Older Persons* (1981).

ISBN 0-313-29277-9

9 780313 292774

EAN

90000>

HARDCOVER BAR CODE